Avoid Disaster, Cut Cost, Protect Your Sh*t!

IT Survival Guide !!!

ALP ISIN

DEDICATION

❖

To my amazing family, my rock and my refuge.

And to Mom, the heart of our home and the wind beneath my wings. Thank you for everything.

In loving memory of my Aunt Canan, whose love and kindness will never be forgotten.

ACKNOWLEDGMENTS

❖

This project has been a journey of three years, and I am deeply grateful to all those who have supported and encouraged me along the way. I am especially thankful to my colleagues and staff for their support and encouragement throughout this project.

As a trusted mentor, Mike has helped me immensely, from guiding me on the book's title to inspiring the cover idea that came to life. I deeply appreciate his wisdom and support.

And to Divyani, whose dedication and hard work were instrumental in bringing this book to fruition. Without your contributions, this book simply wouldn't exist.

WHO SHOULD READ THIS BOOK?

❖

In a world where technology has become the backbone of business operations, small businesses are both blessed and challenged by the digital realm. This book is not just for tech-savvy enthusiasts; it's for everyone navigating the tech landscape. The language here is intentionally light and conversational, ensuring that the complexities of IT are demystified for all readers.

Whether you're a small business owner striving to level the playing field with larger corporations or an aspiring entrepreneur venturing into the competitive marketplace, this book is your guide through the ever-evolving world of technology.

Let's face it - technology can be a double-edged sword. What was once a blessing can quickly turn into a curse when IT-related problems arise. In today's fast-paced digital age, timely resolution is key to avoiding these technological pitfalls.

Small business owners usually expect a lot from technology. When it's doing its job seamlessly, it's often overlooked, but the moment it acts up, frustration kicks in. I am talking about everything from computers and cell phones to internet and software solutions. Now, with over a decade of experience offering IT and tech support to small businesses, I've seen this scenario play out firsthand many times. It's interesting to note that the average user doesn't usually dive into the intricate details of how interconnected and complex IT systems can be. However, when it comes to running a business, that very information can turn out to be crucial! That's where this book swoops in. I want to equip you with the tech-savvy necessary to navigate the digital landscape. No unnecessary jargons, just straight talk. Ever heard the saying, "Knowledge is power"? Well, in the tech world, it's like a superhero cape. You don't need to become a tech genius, but understanding the basics can save your business from disasters.

I'm not here to point fingers, but let's be real - some businesses stumble when it comes to tech and fall flat. I'm here to spill the tea on those pitfalls so you can sidestep them like a pro. And guess what? Your staff and your friendly tech support team will thank you for it.

Your business journey is about to get a whole lot smoother–tech hiccups, be warned!

CONTENTS

Dedication 5

Acknowledgments 7

Who Should Read This Book? 9

Glossary 15

Introduction 23

Why This Book is Important for Your Business 24

What to Expect 25

Chapter 1: 10 Mistakes That All Small Business Owners Make 27

1.1.Watch Out for These Common Mistakes 28

1.2.The Ideal Roadmap for You to Follow 41

Chapter 2: Do you Know the True Cost of IT? 45

2.1.Direct Costs: The Price You Pay 47

2.2.Indirect Costs: The Hidden Toll 49

Chapter 3: Why Should You Do A Risk vs Cost Analysis?   55

    3.1.What is a Risk vs Cost Analysis?   56

    3.2.Why is Risk vs Cost Analysis Important for SMBs?   57

    3.3.How Can You Identify Potential Risks?   57

    3.4.How to Determine Your Risk Tolerance?   60

    3.5. How to Conduct A Risk vs Cost Analysis?   62

Chapter 4: What Scares You?   77

    4.1.Fear #1: Losing All Your Data: 78

    4.2.Fear #2: Damage to Your Reputation: 81

    4.3.Fear #3: Losing Control Over Sensitive Information   83

    4.4.The Key to Conquering Your Fears   85

Chapter 5: Essentials: Your Organization Can't Afford to Overlook   97

    5.1.Essential Password Protocols   100

    5.2.Multi-Factor Authentication: Adding Layers of Security   109

    5.3.Securing Network and Endpoint Devices   117

    5.4.Cybersecurity Training and Awareness for Employees   126

    5.5.The Untold Reality of Cyber Insurance   136

Chapter 6: Challenges Faced by All Small Organizations   139

    6.1.Challenge: Keeping Up with Rapid Technological Change 141

    6.2.Challenge: Managing Data   144

6.3.Challenge: The Need for Up-to-Date Security Measures   144

6.4.Challenge: Which Cloud-based Solutions to Choose?   146

6.5.Challenge: Integrating Systems and Applications   149

6.6.Challenge: Staying Ahead of Cyber Threats   150

6.7.Challenge: Adapting to the Mobile Revolution   156

6.8.Challenge: Managing Remote Teams   158

Chapter 7: Making The Right Choices   161

7.1.Choosing the Right Hardware   163

7.2.Choosing the Right Software   166

7.3.Choosing the Right IT Partner   170

7.4.Making the Right Investment: Business Continuity   175

Conclusion   **181**

IT as a Strategic Investment   182

Moving Forward with Confidence   182

Final Thoughts   183

GLOSSARY

❖

1. Antivirus Software:

Software designed to detect, prevent, and remove malicious software such as viruses, worms, and trojans.

2. Authentication:

The process of verifying the identity of a user or device, typically through usernames, passwords, and other forms of verification such as MFA (Multi-Factor Authentication).

3. Backup:

The process of creating copies of data to protect against loss. It is important to test backups to ensure data recovery in case of disaster.

4. Breach Response:

The steps taken by an organization to respond to and recover from a data breach, including notifying affected parties and taking legal and technical measures to limit damage.

5. Bring Your Own Device (BYOD):

A policy that allows employees to use their personal devices for work purposes, presenting potential security risks if not managed properly.

6. Business Continuity Plan (BCP):

A strategy that ensures a business can continue operations during and after a disaster or major disruption.

7. Cloud Computing:

The use of internet-based services for storing and managing data, which offers flexibility and scalability for businesses.

8. Cyber Insurance:

Insurance designed to mitigate financial losses from cyber incidents such as data breaches or hacking.

9. Cybersecurity:

The practice of protecting systems, networks, and programs from digital attacks. This includes antivirus software, firewalls, and training employees about security risks.

10.Cybersecurity Risks:

Threats posed by hackers, malware, and phishing attacks that can compromise business data and operations.

11.Data Breach:

An incident where sensitive or confidential data is accessed, used, or disclosed without authorization.

12.Data Loss:

The accidental or deliberate destruction of data. Strategies such as regular backups and data protection measures help minimize the risk of data loss.

13.Disaster Recovery Plan (DRP):

A set of procedures designed to restore business operations after an IT disaster, focusing on data restoration and system recovery.

14.Direct Costs:

Immediate expenses associated with IT services, such as hardware purchases and maintenance.

15.Downtime:

Periods when systems are unavailable, often resulting in lost productivity and revenue.

16.Endpoint Protection:

Security measures that protect end-user devices such as computers, smartphones, and tablets from cyber threats.

17.Firewall:

A security system that monitors and controls incoming and outgoing network traffic, forming a barrier between trusted and untrusted networks.

18.Firewall Rule:

Specific instructions configured within a firewall to allow or block specific types of network traffic, adding an extra layer of protection.

19.Hardware:

The physical components of a computer system, including servers, desktops, and laptops.

20.Indirect Costs:

Hidden expenses from IT disruptions, such as reduced productivity or reputational damage.

21.Incident Response Plan:

A predefined set of procedures designed to detect, respond to, and recover from cybersecurity incidents like breaches or system failures.

22.IT Infrastructure:

The combined hardware, software, networks, and systems that support business operations.

23.Legacy Systems:

Older IT systems that may lack current security updates, exposing businesses to cyber risks.

24.Malware:

A general term for malicious software designed to disrupt, damage, or gain unauthorized access to computer systems. Includes viruses, trojans, ransomware, etc.

25.Multi-Factor Authentication (MFA):

An additional layer of security that requires two or more verification methods to gain access to an account.

26.Patch Management:

The process of managing updates for software applications, ensuring security vulnerabilities are addressed promptly through the installation of patches.

27.Password Manager:

A tool for securely storing and managing passwords, reducing the need for individuals to remember multiple complex passwords.

28.Penetration Testing:

A simulated cyber-attack against a system to identify vulnerabilities that could be exploited by hackers. This helps businesses strengthen their defenses.

29.Phishing:

A method of tricking individuals into revealing sensitive information by pretending to be a legitimate entity.

30.Phishing Simulation:

A method used to train employees by mimicking real-world phishing attacks, helping them recognize and avoid such threats in the future.

31.Recovery Point Objective (RPO):

The maximum amount of data that can be lost before it causes unacceptable harm to a business, often used in disaster recovery planning.

32.Recovery Time Objective (RTO):

The targeted duration of time within which a business process must be restored after a disaster to avoid unacceptable consequences.

33.Ransomware:

A type of malware that locks a user out of their system or encrypts data, demanding a ransom to regain access.

34.Risk vs. Cost Analysis:

A method used to evaluate the balance between the potential risks and costs of implementing a security solution or business strategy.

35.Server:

A central computer system that provides services or data to other computers in a network.

36.Software:

The programs and other operating information used by a computer. This includes everything from operating systems to business-specific applications.

37.Software Maintenance:

Regular updates to software systems to fix bugs and improve security.

38.Security Awareness Training:

Programs designed to educate employees on best practices and awareness of potential cybersecurity threats such as phishing and social engineering.

39.Security Patch:

An update to software designed to fix vulnerabilities that could be exploited by cyber attackers.

40.Virtual Private Network (VPN):

A secure connection that allows users to access a private network over a public internet connection, helping protect data and ensure privacy.

41.Virtualization:

The creation of virtual versions of physical hardware resources, such as servers, allowing more efficient resource use.

42.Virus:

A type of malicious software that can replicate itself and spread to other computers, causing damage to systems and files.

43.Vulnerability:

A flaw or weakness in a system that can be exploited to compromise security.

44.Vulnerability Assessment:

A systematic process of identifying, quantifying, and prioritizing vulnerabilities in an IT system, network, or software application.

INTRODUCTION

❖

I n today's digital landscape, small organizations like yours rely more than ever on technology to thrive. Whether it's managing customer relationships, streamlining operations, or securing sensitive data, IT has become the foundation of modern business. Yet, for many small business owners, navigating the complexities of IT can feel overwhelming and risky. With limited resources and the pressure to keep costs down, it's easy to make decisions that can lead to costly mistakes, security vulnerabilities, or missed opportunities.

This book is written for small business owners who want to harness the power of technology without falling into the common pitfalls. Whether you're running a startup or managing an established small organization, *The IT Survival Guide* will show you how to make smart IT investments, avoid costly errors, and protect your organization from cyber threats. Technology should be an asset - not a source of stress. This guide will empower you to make informed IT decisions that improve efficiency, reduce costs, and safeguard your business.

Why This Book is Important for Your Business

You've probably heard the saying, "IT is an investment, not an expense." But what does that truly mean for your organization? It's easy to view IT costs as burdensome, something to trim back wherever possible. However, when approached correctly, IT can transform into a strategic asset that drives long-term savings, enhances productivity, and bolsters security. By understanding the true value of IT, you can make informed decisions that position your business for success - while avoiding expensive mistakes along the way.

This guide will help you:

1. **Avoid Common IT Mistakes:** From buying the wrong equipment to ignoring security risks, small organizations often make preventable errors when it comes to technology. We'll walk through these common mistakes and how to sidestep them.

2. **Cut Costs Without Compromising Quality:** Budget constraints are a reality for every small organization, but cutting corners on IT can lead

to bigger expenses down the road. We'll show you how to find the right balance between cost-saving measures and high-quality solutions.

3. **Stay Secure in a Digital World:** With cybersecurity threats looming larger than ever, small organizations are prime targets. This book will give you practical strategies to protect your business, your data, and your customers.

What to Expect

Throughout this book, you'll find actionable advice, real-world examples, and insights gained from years of experience in helping small organizations navigate their IT challenges. Each chapter is designed to be practical and easy to understand - no technical jargon, just clear and concise guidance that you can apply to your business today.

We'll kick things off by addressing the most frequent IT blunders small business owners make. From there, we'll delve into the true costs of IT - unpacking both direct and hidden expenses - and show you how to conduct a risk versus cost analysis to ensure your investments pay off. Finally, we'll explore essential strategies for cybersecurity and the critical role IT plays in your business's continuity and growth.

By the end of this guide, you'll have the knowledge and tools to make confident IT decisions, cut unnecessary costs, and strengthen your business's security.

Let's get started on your journey to smarter IT solutions.

❖

CHAPTER 1

10 MISTAKES THAT ALL SMALL BUSINESS OWNERS MAKE

Running a business can feel like navigating a maze; there's so much to consider! From company structure and business plans to licenses, legalities, marketing, office space, equipment, recruiting a new staff, taxes, target audience, software solutions, tools - the list goes on endlessly. For small business owners, it's easy to feel overwhelmed amidst the challenges of starting out and losing focus on crucial aspects. One such oversight is ensuring that the technology and equipment used for the business are the right fit.

Sure, every dollar matters when you're launching a new venture. However, skimping on the technology that your company relies on could prove costly in the long run. Small businesses thrive with the right technology, yet there are common mistakes that business owners often make, offsetting the benefits and resulting in losses.

1.1.
Watch Out for
These Common Mistakes

In this section, we will discuss ten of these potential errors that business owners should be mindful of and steer clear of.

1.1.1. Purchasing Cheap Equipment

The first of these mistakes is going out on a limb and purchasing cheap equipment to cut costs. Many small company owners skimp on hardware to save money, but they aren't aware that the price of installing subpar equipment is much greater when you take into account repair expenses, shorter lifespans, data corruption, and downtime. As my grandfather used to say, "I am not rich enough to buy cheap things." Well, this classic saying becomes very relevant once you realize it has only been six months since you bought your new device, and it has already started to slow down and malfunction. It's essential to recognize that not all equipment is suitable for commercial use. The commercial equipment might be expensive upfront, but they are designed for efficiency and to last or take the abuse of daily professional usage.

When it comes to electronic devices like computers or laptops, it's crucial to make the right choice for the long haul. Computers are more than just tools; they're the backbone of business operations. Compromising on the quality of these essential devices can lead to performance issues and a decline in productivity among employees, ultimately affecting revenue.

Lower-end devices tend to degrade faster, contributing to decreased efficiency and, consequently, financial losses. Running mission-critical programs on commercial-grade hardware is essential for sustained performance. If budget constraints are a concern, exploring credit and lease options for IT equipment is a viable solution.

One common mistake is focusing solely on the immediate cost without considering the overall expenses associated with subpar hardware. Costs for maintenance, repairs, and frequent replacements quickly accumulate, especially when factoring in the revenue loss during downtime for repairs or replacements. In the end, the supposed savings from cheaper hardware can easily be outweighed by these hidden costs.

1.1.2. Running the Business with BYOD Equipment

Let's break this down in plain talk. So, here's a classic mistake many companies make - letting their employees hook up their computers and gadgets to the business network with zero restrictions. You see this a lot in young, tech-savvy firms where everyone is seen as a bit of a tech expert. Small business owners love the whole BYOD (Bring Your Own Device) gig to dodge the cost of buying company computers. Sounds like a plan, right? Well, not so fast.

Sure, big-shot companies let employees bring their own gear to the office, but they've got some serious guardrails in place. Now, here's the catch with BYOD - it might save some bucks, but it's like leaving the back door wide open for potential cyber trouble. Why? 'Cause when everyone's rolling with their own gadgets, company data is chilling on all sorts of unsecured devices, often without any fancy encryption. That's a recipe for data breaches and a serious legal headache.

And don't get me started on viruses crashing the company network through a personal laptop with about as much security as a cardboard box. Or the new recruit rocking a pirated version of the software, thinking they're being helpful. Oops.

Another problem with BYOD is that employees might be using non-commercial licensed software for business purposes, which poses potential legal and security issues. Tech firms release home and professional versions of their software and gear for a reason: less expensive, scaled-down home versions are simply against the license agreement, which makes it illegal. Your ISP-provided / home Wi-Fi router may seem to be acceptable, but they are not designed to be used in a business environment. These products are designed with low cost and attractive features in mind rather than reliability and security.

Any company, no matter how big or small, should invest in business-class IT to succeed. Even though professional equipment often may not seem financially feasible for a small business, it is important to keep in mind the risks one could incur by not investing in it.

1.1.3. Overextending the Technology Life Span

Computers and tech age faster than we might think. Every three to five years, your once cutting-edge tech becomes outdated with new breakthroughs in

IT. Given the ever-changing tech landscape, keeping your business competitive means embracing updates and upgrades. But, upgrading can seem like a financial headache, leading some to delay until it's absolutely necessary - like when the hardware calls it quits.

From a budget standpoint, it might seem logical to wait until an upgrade is imperative. However, clinging to outdated technology could end up costing your business more in the long run. Older gear and software can hamper productivity, lead to data loss, and create compatibility issues with future advancements, not to mention exposing your business to security threats.

When a piece of hardware or software hits its "End of Life" (EOL), manufacturers stop producing and selling it. Beyond that point, they no longer provide patches or security upgrades. This leaves these devices or software vulnerable to cyberattacks. Known issues without patches become open doors for cybercriminals to exploit, gaining access to systems and potentially compromising other devices or systems.

1.1.4. Careless & Incautious Password Generation and Storage

Alright, let's talk about a major headache for almost all small businesses - weak passwords. Numerous small companies utilize different cloud-based services, each of which calls for a distinct account. Now, the catch is financial details and super-sensitive data often chill in these systems. If employees are rocking weak or same-old passwords across different accounts, it's like hanging a "Hack Me" sign.

And get this - some employees might not even realize the risk they're putting their organizations in. A study by Yubico spilled the tea: around 54% of industry folks reuse passwords on different work accounts. Oh, and a chunk, 42% to be exact, still jot down their passwords. Even big shots like C-level executives and business owners are involved in this risky business. (Yubico, 2021)[1] Danger zone, right?

Now, cybercriminals aren't exactly sitting around twiddling their thumbs. They've got these high-speed apps ready to zip through passwords, especially the ones people tend to use, like birthdays or Fido's name. Hashing is another trick they pull, like Pass-the-Hash (PtH), where they grab a password hash and use it like a magic key to waltz into systems and go all Sherlock across your networks.

But fear not! Building a fortress against these cyber sneak attacks starts with a pep talk for your staff. Educate them on the ABCs of safe data practices - no falling for phishing emails and definitely no wimpy passwords.

---

[1] https://www.helpnetsecurity.com/2021/06/10/employees-reuse-passwords-across-multiple-work-accounts/

Throw in a trusty password manager to keep things organized, and voila! Unique and complex passwords for every site. It's like your own secret weapon. And here's a pro tip: switch up those passwords often, don't recycle them on different sites, and throw in some MFA (Multi-factor Authentication) for good measure. The more secure your passcode, the more robust your protection from potential cyberattacks.

1.1.5. Overlooking Exposure to Cyberthreats

Cyber threats are the ultimate nemesis for small businesses. I am talking trojans, viruses, ransomware - the whole villainous gang of cyber threats. These are the codes crafted by cybercriminals to sneak into your networks, swipe your info, or, worse, hold your data hostage. It's the digital Wild West out there.

These nasty bugs can infiltrate your gadgets through infected devices, shady emails, or sketchy websites, causing chaos. For small businesses, this can mean shelling out big bucks for repairs or replacements, a real headache. Plus, it opens the door wide for hackers to stroll in and play with your data, putting everyone at risk – clients and staff included.

Now, let's talk about defense strategy. Businesses armed with top-notch tech defenses can slash the risk of these cyber sneak attacks. And that's where Endpoint Protection systems come into play. They shield devices from virus threats and give the bosses a control center to keep tabs on security updates for everyone. But wait, there's more! Web security is another key player, blocking users from diving into dangerous websites and downloading nasty malware.

So, here's the battle plan: anti-virus software, malware protection, a robust firewall, and solid policies to lock down your fortress. Trust me, you can't play hide and seek with cyber threats. Make your IT security the guardian of your business story right from the start before things start spiraling south.

1.1.6. No Reliable Backup

Losing crucial data is like hitting your business with a one-two punch—work efficiency drops, customers get frustrated, everyday operations go haywire, and your revenue takes a hit. That's where the superhero move of data backup comes into play.

Data loss can strike in various forms - device glitches, ransomware attacks, oops moments, disasters, or even a good old-fashioned theft. But fear not because data backup is the knight in shining armor that can rescue your information. It's like a safety net, stored in a secure, separate spot, far away from the original device.

However, many companies fail to consistently perform regular data backups, and even when they do, they often neglect the critical step of testing these backups. This oversight can have significant consequences. While bigger businesses usually have their IT wizards keeping an eye on backups, small businesses, wearing all the hats, might not prioritize it. Some, if they have a backup, might start feeling invincible, thinking it's just a useless chore. Worse yet, some small businesses skip the backup gig altogether, assuming everything will magically work.

Sure, creating a solid backup plan takes time and a bit of cash, but it's a small price to pay compared to the chaos of recreating lost data from scratch. So, let's not play with fire—back up your data, folks!

1.1.7. Forgetting Software Maintenance

Software upgrades are essential for any business owner looking to keep their company ahead of the competition. From operating systems to office applications, accounting software, and industry-specific apps, these different types of software must be updated according to their respective timetables.

Now, here's where some business owners take a detour into the danger zone by giving the cold shoulder to these upgrades. Big mistake. Why? Because when a software upgrade hits the scene, it's like a rockstar makeover. It becomes more efficient, supercharged, and ready to tackle all the needs your business throws at it. It's the new and improved version, with fancy features, better tools, speedier performance, and bug fixes—the whole shebang. And the cherry on top? It patches up any weak spots in security from the past, keeping your business fortress secure from cyber baddies.

Using outdated software platforms may expose your company to unpatched security weaknesses, making it easier for hackers to gain access to your system or network. Therefore, it is crucial to regularly check for the latest security patches and updates. However, it's important not to test these new patches yourself. Consulting with your IT partner on when to install these fixes is recommended.

When it's time to bid farewell to the old and usher in the new, you've got options. Think SaaS and Cloud Computing - these heavy hitters offer a bunch of perks to keep your business shining. But hey, I get it - diving into these options can feel like finding your way through an intricate puzzle. That's why having an expert by your side is key. Let them be your guide through the upgrade adventure. It's worth it to keep that business of yours at the top of its game.

1.1.8. Not Knowing About Hardware Updates Required with Changing Software

It's important to keep your software updated, but you must also pay close attention to your hardware. You see, when developers design and release new software, they utilize the latest technological advancements in hardware and infrastructure to accomplish the improvements. That means your old faithful hardware might not be BFFs with the fresh software or might struggle to handle all its cool features.

So, here's the deal - if you want your software to be the star of the show, your hardware needs to be its trusty sidekick. Yes, I know, the idea of investing in new hardware can sound a bit intimidating, like facing a dragon in a game. But guess what? It's a crucial step to level up your computing experience.

Remember, your hardware and software are like the dynamic duo of the tech world. They team up to give you a smooth, seamless computing ride. Make sure they're on the same page, and you'll be soaking in all the goodness of the latest tech magic. Upgrade that hardware, keep the software smiling, and enjoy a tech-savvy adventure!

1.1.9. Skipping User Training

Alright, let's paint a scenario here: You've dropped a pretty penny on this game-changing software to supercharge your work. But when it comes to the user training program, you give it a pass, thinking your team can figure out the app on their own—who needs to spend extra cash, right? Fast forward to Monday, and your staff is deep in the struggle, trying to decode the mysteries of the application instead of getting actual work done. The week ticks by, and they're still not buddy-buddy with all the software features, using it like a distant cousin. A month zooms past, and instead of mastering the new app, they're back to their old tricks, sticking to what they know. So, that amazing app you bought to skyrocket revenue? It's practically on vacation because your team can't make the most of it. Could've dodged this whole mess by factoring in training costs when you bought the software—just saying.

Access to help and training when needed is crucial not only for fixing a problem but also for onboarding a new employee. Depending on your organization, you might have a point person who is well-versed in your company software and can help train new users. Whether you are a small team or a large organization, your team needs to be familiar with your IT policies and procedures.

Having security awareness training as well as IT policy procedure training as part of a new employee onboarding is crucial. This training can be completed with internal resources or by your IT partner. Additionally, it is best practice to do refresher training on a regular basis to update the employees on new threats as well as possible changes that might be coming.

1.1.10 Taking IT Support from Under-Qualified and Non-Certified People

Most owners of small businesses and entrepreneurs lack the funds necessary to hire a professional IT team, and they end up hiring a tech-savvy family member or a neighbor to administer their IT infrastructure. Or better yet, oftentimes, they try to do everything themselves, thinking, *how hard can it be to run a computer?* Spoiler alert: it can be trickier than it seems.

Unfortunately, many of these DIY IT enthusiasts lack the magic combo of knowledge and skills needed to keep the tech ship sailing smoothly. As a business owner, should your focus really be on becoming an IT expert? Probably not. And let's be real, hiring someone who's not up to snuff in the tech department is like asking your cousin's friend's roommate to fix your spaceship - not the best idea.

Why? Because down the road, you might end up forking out more cash just to fix the mess left by someone not quite qualified for the job. If you're thinking of getting some outside help for your tech game, here's the secret code: demand qualifications, certifications, and references. A legit IT pro will have the training and certifications to navigate the tech jungle, seeing the bigger picture and understanding the consequences of every move on your IT setup.

So, long story short, don't DIY your IT if it's not your jam, and definitely don't hire someone who's not up to snuff. Get yourself a certified IT professional who knows their stuff, and you'll save yourself headaches and cash down the line.

1.2.
The Ideal Roadmap
for You to Follow

In the grand scheme of running a small business, navigating the complexities of technology can be like solving a puzzle with many interconnected pieces. As we've explored the common mistakes that small business owners often make, it's crucial to recognize the importance of getting the technology puzzle right from the start. Here are the key actions that businesses should take:

1. Consult the IT Expert: Begin your journey by seeking advice from IT experts when starting your business. A comprehensive assessment will help identify your specific needs, ensuring a tailored technology solution.

2. Find the Right Software: Invest time and effort in finding the right software for your business. Consider your operational requirements, scalability, and compatibility to make informed

decisions that align with your long-term goals.

3. Ensure Proper Hardware: Recognize the value of investing in quality hardware. Commercial-grade equipment may be more expensive initially, but its efficiency and durability make it a wise investment that pays off in the long run.

4. Prioritize Cybersecurity: Make cybersecurity a top priority. Implement robust endpoint protection, web security measures, and sound policies to safeguard your business from the ever-evolving landscape of cyber threats.

5. Plan for Business Continuity: Develop a reliable backup strategy to safeguard against data loss, ensuring your business can quickly recover from unforeseen events such as device glitches, ransomware attacks, or disasters.

6. Regular Maintenance and Updates: Commit to ongoing maintenance and updates for both hardware and software. Don't overlook the importance of staying current to enhance efficiency, address security vulnerabilities, and extend the lifespan of your technology assets.

7. Manage the Lifecycle: Implementing a robust strategy for maintaining the lifecycle of both hardware and software is paramount. This involves not only understanding the lifecycle

of your technology but also incorporating changes effectively. Develop a well-thought-out budgeting plan that aligns with the expected lifespan of your equipment, preventing overextension and ensuring a seamless transition when updates or replacements are necessary. This proactive approach guarantees that your business remains equipped with up-to-date and efficient technology without compromising financial stability.

By taking these actions, businesses can set a solid foundation for their technological endeavors, paving the way for efficiency, security, and sustainable growth. After all, in the world of small business, the right technology choices can make all the difference.

CHAPTER 2

❖

DO YOU KNOW THE
TRUE COST OF IT?

Technology has become an essential component of modern business operations. Whether you're a small startup or a medium-sized player, chances are you're throwing some serious cash into your IT setup. I mean, in 2021, a whopping 91% of small and medium-sized businesses game invested in tech, averaging around $118,000[2]. That's no pocket change! Fast forward to today, and these numbers continue to underscore the financial commitment businesses are making to keep pace with the demands of the digital era.

These figures serve as a reminder: technology investments are not merely a trend; they are an integral part of a business's financial landscape. However, navigating the realm of IT spending without a clear understanding of its true cost can impact budgetary allocations and, ultimately, the bottom line.

So, in this chapter, we're about to unravel the mystery of the true cost of IT. We'll break down the dollars and cents, and by the end of it, you'll have a clear picture of how your organization's financial performance is dancing with the tune of your tech investments.

---

2   https://www.bdc.ca/en/about/mediaroom/news-releases/small-medium-sized-businesses-that-invest-digital-technologies-more-competitive-bdc-study#:~:text=Key%20findings%3A,businesses%20use%20digital%20technologies%20effectively.

2.1.
Direct Costs:
The Price You Pay

Direct costs are the expenses that are directly related to the implementation and use of technology in your business. Here are some of the examples that fall into this category:

- Hardware: You know, the physical stuff – computers, servers, printers, firewalls, all those techy gadgets that make up your IT world.

- Software: Now, we're talking the digital side – Microsoft 365, Sage, Quickbooks, Adobe, AutoCAD, EsiLaw, PC Law, and whatever else your computers are running.

Maintenance and support: The ongoing expenses for keeping the show running smoothly. Think hardware repairs, software updates, security patches, and the lifesavers we call technical support.

2.1.1. How Do You Keep Direct Costs in Check?

I. Plan ahead: When making decisions about technology investments, it's important to consider not only the upfront cost but also the ongoing costs associated with maintaining and supporting the technology. Make sure you have a clear understanding of the total cost of ownership before making any decisions.

II.   Shop around: When making purchasing decisions, it's essential to consider the price versus value of the product or service rather than simply choosing the cheapest option. Comparing prices and negotiating with vendors is a good practice to ensure you're getting the most for your budget. Value-based pricing is a helpful concept to keep in mind as you make these decisions, as it emphasizes the importance of considering the overall value a product or service provides rather than simply looking at its cost.

III. Monitor usage: Make sure you're monitoring your technology usage to ensure that you're getting the most value for your money. For example, if you have software licenses that you're not using, you may want to consider canceling them to reduce your expenses.

IV.   Consider seeking external expertise: If you don't have the necessary in-house expertise to manage your IT infrastructure, it will be beneficial to seek external help to address some or all of your IT needs. This can help you reduce your direct IT costs by taking advantage of expert knowledge and tapping into the economies of scale of external providers. Remember that bit we talked about earlier? As a business owner, it's super important to avoid the mistake of hiring unqualified individuals to handle your IT infrastructure. Rather, it's recommended that you seek out competent IT professionals who have the training and the necessary experience to understand the bigger picture and the consequences of their actions on your overall IT infrastructure. So, don't be shy about asking for their credentials and references!

2.2.
Indirect Costs:
The Hidden Toll

Let's shine a light on the not-so-obvious expenses that come hand-in-hand with your tech game—aka the indirect costs. These are the ones that don't scream, "Hi, I'm an IT expense!" right off the bat. We're talking about the bills that dance around the edges, like energy costs, downtime expenses, lost productivity, decreased employee satisfaction, and potential turnover.

Moving beyond the surface, let's explore the intricate details of calculating indirect costs. It goes beyond simple numerical figures; it involves uncovering the hidden expenses that accumulate quietly and impact your business.

Consider a scenario where you're running a retail shoe store with 5 employees. While they actively engage with your point-of-sale system and inventory management software, any downtime in the computer network can bring your retail operation to a standstill, resulting in significant financial losses.

Here's the math: If each of your awesome employees costs you an average of $25 per hour, and you lose 2 hours of sales in a day due to downtime, that's a daily hit of $250 ($25 x 2 hours x 5 employees). Now, stretch that over 10 days of downtime in a year, and you're looking at $2,500 ($250 x 10 days). But that's not the whole story.

Let's talk about the sales you might lose during downtime. If, on average, you lose 15 sales each day of downtime, and they usually spend $100 each, you're looking at an additional cost of $15,000 ($100 x 10 x 15). Suddenly, your indirect costs just got a little heftier.

But wait, there's more. Beyond lost sales and wages, there are other sneaky costs creeping in. How about the overhead costs, like rent, utilities, insurance, and maintenance fees - the bills don't take a holiday just because your business is on pause.

Another significant impact can be on customer trust and loyalty. Customers who experience poor service due to downtime, especially if it's a recurring issue, may become frustrated and take their business elsewhere. Winning back these customers' trust requires effort, potentially through discounts, promotions, or improved services. However, this process can be slow, costly, and not always successful.

And let's not forget about the intangible costs. Downtime isn't just a cold, hard number; it significantly impacts the morale of your employees. Their job satisfaction takes a nosedive, engagement drops, and before you know it, they're waving goodbye, leading to high turnover rates. Replacing them becomes not just a time investment but also money down the drain, along with a potential hit to your customer service quality.

The true cost of IT is a Sherlock Holmes game - you have to look beyond the obvious. It's not just the price tag on hardware and software; it's the indirect costs, the frustration, the low retention rates, and the impact on overall business success.

Now, why should you care about these behind-the-scenes players? Well, they might seem like small fry, but they can gang up on your profits really quick. These indirect costs are sly. They don't always show up with neon signs. That's why it's crucial to keep a hawk eye on all aspects of your expenditures, both the direct and the sneaky indirect ones. Efficiency is the name of the game. Spot where you might be throwing money out the window and make some savvy adjustments.

And here's a tip for the road: considering a Managed IT Services Provider (MSP) for small to mid-size businesses is a wise move. An MSP brings a buffet of IT services - technical support, software upgrades, security monitoring - to optimize your IT systems. Plus, you get the firepower of a larger IT organization, making the true cost of IT more manageable.

A recent study has highlighted that indirect expenses have experienced a more rapid increase compared to direct costs in previous years[3]. This trend can be attributed to various factors, including fluctuating market conditions, changes in supply chain dynamics, and the evolving nature of operational requirements. The implications of this shift are multifaceted, affecting budgetary considerations, resource allocation, and the overall cost structure of businesses. Therefore, business leaders and financial decision-makers need to be cognizant of this emerging pattern and its potential ramifications.

2.2.1. How to Tackle Indirect Costs Like a Pro?

Here are some steps you can take to minimize indirect IT costs and maximize your IT investment:

---

3   https://www150.statcan.gc.ca/n1/pub/36-28-0001/2023006/article/00005-eng.htm

I.   Conduct an IT cost audit: A thorough IT cost audit can help you understand the full scope of your indirect IT costs and identify areas where you can make changes.

II. Upgrade to energy-efficient equipment: By investing in energy-efficient IT equipment, you can reduce energy costs and minimize the impact of indirect IT costs on your bottom line.

III. Employee Training Programs: Insufficiently trained employees may require more time to accomplish tasks, potentially leading to additional indirect costs for your business. Thus, it's recommended to allocate resources towards ongoing training initiatives to enhance your employees' IT competencies. Furthermore, a proficiently trained workforce is less likely to make errors, consequently mitigating the risk of issues arising and the subsequent expenses incurred.

A comprehensive study conducted by IBM emphasizes the significance of managing indirect IT costs. This research revealed that these concealed costs can account for a substantial 40% to 50% of a business's total IT costs[4]. Yeah, you read that right.

---

4   https://www.ibm.com/downloads/cas/DG7NY5QW

IT costs should not be taken lightly. Know what they are, why they matter, and how to play the game smartly. Maximize your IT investment, cut those indirect costs, keep your team happy and productive, and watch your business success soar. It's not just about the tech; it's about the whole strategy.

❖

CHAPTER 3

WHY SHOULD YOU DO A RISK VS COST ANALYSIS?

As an entrepreneur managing a small business, you're probably always looking for ways to maximize your profits while minimizing your costs. And when it comes to investing in technology, you're likely considering whether the benefits of doing so are worth the investment. But have you considered the risks that come along with that investment? The potential consequences of not investing in technology, or not investing in the right technology, can be devastating to your business. That's why it's so important to do a risk vs. cost analysis before making any major IT investments.

3.1.
What is a Risk vs Cost Analysis?

A risk vs cost analysis serves as your exclusive backstage pass, allowing you to compare the expenses linked to potential risks with the costs associated with mitigating those risks. In the context of IT investments, it's a way of weighing the risks that can affect or disrupt your business against the costs of using the right technology. The goal is to help you make an informed decision about the best technology investments for your business based on your risk tolerance and profit goals.

3.2.
Why is Risk vs Cost Analysis Important for SMBs?

Small businesses are particularly vulnerable to the risks associated with IT investments. According to a study, nearly 60% of small businesses that experience a major data loss go out of business within 6 months[5]. This data underlines the brutal reality that IT risks aren't just about inconvenient setbacks; they're survival challenges. Understanding these risks isn't an optional extra; it's a must-have toolkit for any small business navigating the technology landscape. It's not enough to simply look at the costs of technology and make a decision based on that alone. You need to understand the risks involved and determine whether they're acceptable, given your business goals and risk tolerance.

3.3.
How Can You Identify Potential Risks?

Business risks are unique to each organization and can be influenced by various factors, such as the size of the business, its location, and the industry it operates in. Additionally, the nature of the products or services offered, supply chain complexity, and

---

5   https://www.forbes.com/sites/emilsayegh/2022/08/16/businesses-shutting-down-business/?sh=3718c4614cc6

regulatory environment can also affect the level of risk an organization may face. It's essential to identify these factors that can affect your operations and determine potential risks to your organization. This way, you can easily develop effective strategies to mitigate these risks. Although every organization may have its own set of risks, there are some general ones that you should consider:

- **Cybersecurity Risks:**

This is one of the most significant threats facing small businesses, as cyber-attacks are becoming more common and sophisticated. A cyber-attack can result in data theft, financial loss, and damage to the business's reputation. For instance, a medical clinic that stores patient records and sensitive medical information electronically may face risks such as unauthorized access to patient files. Patient records contain sensitive personal information such as provincial health number, date of birth, addresses, and medical histories. When all these pieces of personal information are combined, the risk of identifying the individual becomes even more pronounced. If this information is accessed by unauthorized parties, it could be used for identity theft, insurance fraud, or sold on the dark web, resulting in financial liabilities for the clinic. 41% of Canadian small businesses that suffered a cyber-attack reported that it cost them at least $100,000[6]. By investing in cybersecurity measures such as firewalls, antivirus software, and intrusion detection systems, your organization can reduce the risks of cyber-attacks, data breaches, and other malicious activities, making it less likely to be targeted.

- **Operational Risks:**

These refer to risks that arise from internal processes and procedures, such as employee error, system failures, or power outages. With the help of proper IT infrastructure and support, businesses can reduce the risk of system failures, downtime, and other operational issues. For instance, investing in business continuity can help ensure that critical business data is not lost in the event of system failures or other disasters.

- **Compliance Risks:**

These risks are associated with legal or regulatory requirements. Organizations that handle sensitive personal information must comply with privacy regulations such as PIPEDA or GDPR. Failure to comply with these regulations can result in significant financial penalties and damage to the business's reputation.

---

6   https://www.theglobeandmail.com/life/adv/article-steep-rise-in-cy-bersecurity-risks-challenges-canadian-organizations/

- **Financial Risks:**

This includes the potential for financial loss or profit impact, often seen when organizations hastily invest in emerging technologies simply because they are trending, without proper guidance from tech experts. For instance, if a retail company invests heavily in a new e-commerce platform without thoroughly understanding its functionality or scalability to meet customer demands, it could result in operational inefficiencies and decreased sales rather than the intended boost. This also underscores the significance of tech expertise in guiding investments toward areas that align with the organization's strategic goals, minimizing financial risks, and ensuring a more sustainable growth trajectory.

3.4.
How to Determine Your Risk Tolerance?

Before you can do a risk vs cost analysis, you need to determine your risk tolerance. This will help you understand what risks you're willing to accept and what risks you're not willing to accept. A good way to do this is to create a risk appetite scale.

A risk appetite scale ranges from zero, meaning you're not willing to accept any risk despite potential opportunities or benefits, to high, meaning you're willing to accept significant risk equal to the possible benefits.

| 0 | Low | Moderate | High |
| (Risk Aversion) | Risk Appetite | Risk Appetite | Risk Appetite |

- 0 to Low: Unwilling to accept any risk, even if it means missing potential opportunities or benefits.

- Low to Moderate: Willing to accept some risk, but only if the potential benefits outweigh the drawbacks.

- Moderate to High: Open to taking significant risks, balancing potential benefits against potential downsides.

- High: Willing to accept substantial risk equal to the possible benefits.

Let's discuss an example here so that you can figure out how to use this risk appetite scale. Think of the risks a law firm might encounter. First, *compliance risks*, integral to the legal profession, could demand a **zero-risk appetite** for strict adherence. *Cybersecurity risks* - with the critical nature of safeguarding client information, a law firm could position itself at a **Low-risk appetite**. *Operational risks*, like system downtime and employee errors, might warrant a **Low to Moderate risk appetite**. *Reputational risks*, given the industry's reliance on trust, might also prompt a low to m**oderate risk appetite**. *Strategic risks*, aligning with long-term goals, could be met with a **Moderate risk appetite**. Finally, *Financial risks* impacting profitability may be met with a **Moderate to High-risk appetite** for calculated moves.

3.5.
How to Conduct
A Risk vs Cost Analysis?

Now that you've established your risk tolerance, conducting a thorough risk vs cost analysis becomes the key to making informed decisions about your IT investments. Here's a step-by-step guide on how to proceed:

1. Identify Risks:

- We've just covered this, but let's review again: identifying potential risks is a crucial step in making an informed investment decision. This involves considering various types of risks, such as cybersecurity threats, compliance issues, and other operational risks that can affect your business. Additionally, it can be helpful to research the most common risks faced by businesses in your industry and how they can impact your organization.

2. Prioritize Risks:

- Prioritize these risks based on their potential impact and likelihood of occurrence. Some risks may have severe consequences but are less likely, while others may be more common but less damaging.

- Begin by evaluating the potential consequences each risk could have on your business if it were to materialize. This includes considering the financial, operational, reputational, and strategic impacts. Use a scale from 1 to 10 to rate the potential impact of each risk, with 1 being minimal and 10 being significant, in alignment with your risk tolerance levels. Ask questions such as: How severe would the impact be on our finances, considering our risk appetite? What effect would it have on our operations and ability to deliver products/services, given our tolerance for operational disruptions? Would it damage our reputation with customers, partners, or stakeholders, and how does this align with our risk threshold? Does it threaten our long-term strategic goals and market position, and is this within the acceptable range of risks based on our risk tolerance? This evaluation ensures that the consequences of each risk are viewed through the lens of your organization's risk tolerance, providing a more nuanced understanding of their potential impact on your business objectives.

- Next, analyze the probability or likelihood of each risk event occurring. This involves considering historical data, industry trends, expert opinions, and internal assessments. Assign a probability value to each risk, typically between 0 and 1, with 0 representing no chance of occurrence and 1 indicating certainty. For example, A risk with a probability of 0.8 (or 80%) means there's a high likelihood of it happening. However, a risk with a probability of 0.3 (or 30%) suggests a moderate chance of occurrence. Furthermore, a risk with a probability of 0.1 (or 10%) indicates a low likelihood but not impossible.

- Multiply the potential impact by the likelihood of occurrence for each risk to calculate its risk priority or risk score. The formula is simple:

*** Risk Priority = Impact × Probability**

For example, if a risk has a potential impact score of 8 (on a scale of 1 to 10) and a probability of 0.5, its risk priority would be:

Risk Priority = 8 (Impact) × 0.5 (Probability) = 4.

The higher the risk priority score, the more critical the risk is to address.

Once you have calculated the risk priority for each identified risk, sort them in descending order of their scores. This will create a ranked list of risks, with the most critical ones at the top. You can then focus your attention on mitigating or managing the top-ranked risks first.

3. Quantify Cost of Risks:

- Quantify the cost of each identified risk by assessing the financial impact it could have on your business. Include potential losses, additional expenses, and any long-term future impacts.

4. Evaluate Risk Mitigation Strategies:

- For each identified risk, develop and evaluate potential mitigation strategies. Consider how certain technologies, practices, or policies can minimize the likelihood and impact of each risk.

- Assess the costs associated with implementing these risk mitigation strategies and factor them into your overall cost analysis.

5. Compare Investment Costs with Benefits:

- Evaluate the costs alongside the expected benefits of the IT investment. This involves evaluating both the quantitative and qualitative advantages that the technology solution offers, such as increased operational efficiency, enhanced customer experience, competitive advantage, or potential market expansion.

- Ensure that the benefits outweigh the costs associated with implementing these risk mitigation strategies to justify the investment.

6. Document and Communicate Findings:

- Clearly document the results of your risk vs cost analysis. Create a comprehensive report that outlines identified risks, associated costs, and risk mitigation strategies.

- Communicate these findings with key stakeholders, ensuring everyone involved understands the decision-making process and the rationale behind the chosen course of action.

7. Iterative Process:

Understand that risk vs cost analysis is not a one-time task. As your business evolves and the technology landscape changes, regularly revisit and update your analysis to adapt to new risks and opportunities. Keep in mind that the risks you face today may not be the same tomorrow, and the benefits you seek might require a recalibration of your risk appetite.

3.5.1. Case Study: Applying Risk vs Cost Analysis in Real Business Scenarios

Let's look at an example to illustrate the importance and process of conducting a risk vs cost analysis. Consider a fictional scenario of a local pharmacy, "HealthFirst."

Scenario Overview:

In a bustling neighborhood, nestled among local businesses, lies "HealthFirst Pharmacy," a trusted community pharmacy known for its personalized care and commitment to patient well-being. The owner, Maria, recognizes the need to modernize operations through a new technology investment. To make an informed decision, she follows a thorough risk vs cost analysis process to identify potential risks, prioritize them, and evaluate how investing in technology can mitigate these risks.

Identifying Risks:

- Cybersecurity Risks: Risks include potential data breaches of patient information, leading to legal and reputational damage.

- Operational Risks: Challenges such as system failures during prescription processing, resulting in customer dissatisfaction and loss of revenue.

- Compliance Risks: Non-compliance with healthcare regulations could lead to hefty fines and loss of accreditation.

Prioritizing Risks:

Maria assigns impact scores to each risk based on its potential consequences:

- **Cybersecurity Threats:**

Impact Assessment: Maria assesses the potential impact of a cybersecurity breach on the pharmacy's operations and reputation. She considers the financial costs associated with data recovery, legal fees, and the loss of customer trust.

Impact Score: Maria rates the impact of cybersecurity threats as 9 out of 10, indicating a high potential for severe financial and reputational damage.

- **Operational Risks:**

Impact Assessment: Maria evaluates the potential impact of system failures during prescription processing. She considers the financial loss due to disrupted operations, customer dissatisfaction, and the impact on the pharmacy's ability to serve patients.

Impact Score: Maria rates the impact of operational risks as 8 out of 10, indicating significant financial and operational consequences.

- **Compliance Challenges:**

Impact Assessment: Maria considers the potential impact of non-compliance with healthcare regulations. She evaluates the financial penalties and reputational damage associated with this risk.

Impact Score: Maria rates the impact of compliance challenges as 7 out of 10, recognizing the legal and reputational ramifications of non-compliance with data protection laws.

She then evaluates the likelihood of each risk occurring:

- **Cybersecurity Risk:**

Maria reviews industry reports, cybersecurity trends, and the pharmacy's current security measures. Based on this analysis, she assigns a probability score of 0.8, indicating a high chance of a cybersecurity threat occurring.

- **Operational Risk:**

Maria considers past instances of system failures, the reliability of the pharmacy's current systems, and potential human errors. She assigns a probability score of 0.5, indicating a moderate chance of operational disruptions.

Compliance Risk: Maria reviews healthcare regulations, the pharmacy's adherence history, and the complexity of compliance requirements. She gives a probability score of 0.3, indicating a moderate likelihood of facing compliance challenges.

Calculating Risk Priority Scores:

- Cybersecurity Risk: Risk Priority = 9 (Impact) × 0.8 (Probability) = 7.2

- Operational Risk: Risk Priority = 8 (Impact) × 0.5 (Probability) = 4

- Compliance Risk: Risk Priority = 7 (Impact) × 0.3 (Probability) = 2.1

Quantifying Cost of Risks:

Maria estimates the financial implications of each risk:

- Cybersecurity Risk: Maria estimates the cost of cybersecurity risk by considering potential data breach recovery costs, legal fees, and fines, totaling a minimum of $100,000. This calculation includes the expenses associated with data recovery efforts, legal consultations, and regulatory penalties that could result from a breach.

- Operational Risk: In evaluating operational risks, Maria estimates a potential revenue loss of

$60,000 per year due to system downtime. This calculation considers the average daily revenue of $12,000, assuming a downtime of five days in a year. Additionally, Maria accounts for the wages of five technicians and two pharmacists during the downtime, totaling approximately $9,250 per year. This includes the technicians' hourly wage of $27 and the pharmacist's hourly wage of $52, each working a 10-hour day. Beyond the tangible costs, Maria acknowledges the intangible costs, such as damage to customer trust and brand reputation, which could further impact long-term revenue streams and business sustainability. Furthermore, Maria also considers the overhead costs, including utilities, insurance, licenses, and rent, which would continue to accrue during downtime and further add to the financial impact on the pharmacy.

- Compliance Risk: Potential Maria estimates the cost of compliance risks in British Columbia by considering potential fines, legal fees, and the cost of implementing compliance measures, ranging from $10,000 to $200,000. This estimation involves reviewing healthcare regulations specific to the province, evaluating the complexity of compliance requirements, and consulting with legal experts.

Evaluating Management Strategies:

Maria researches technology solutions that can reduce these risks:

- Cybersecurity Measures: Investment: $25,000

Ensuring all systems and software are regularly updated with the latest security patches and fixes for known vulnerabilities.

Deploying robust antivirus software across all devices to detect and remove malware, ransomware, and other malicious threats.

Implementing MDR services to continuously monitor network traffic, detect suspicious activities, and respond swiftly to potential cyber threats.

Installing and configuring a dedicated firewall to monitor incoming and outgoing network traffic, block unauthorized access, and enhance overall network security.

Enhancing email security measures to protect against phishing attacks, spam, and other email-borne threats.

- **Operational Measures:** Investment: $35,000
    - o Implementing a reliable pharmacy management system to streamline operations, enhance accuracy, and improve efficiency.

- o Implementing a robust backup solution to ensure data integrity and minimize downtime in the event of system failures.

- Compliance Measures: Investment: $3,000

  - o Utilization of compliance management software to track regulations.

  - o Implementation of regular audits and assessments to ensure adherence.

  - o Training employees on data protection and privacy protocols.

Cost vs. Benefit Analysis:

In evaluating the investment in technology solutions for HealthFirst Pharmacy, Maria conducts a thorough cost vs benefit analysis to ensure the decision aligns with the pharmacy's objectives and risk tolerance.

Cybersecurity Measures: Recognizing the critical nature of safeguarding patient data and maintaining the pharmacy's reputation, Maria is considering an investment of $25,000 in cybersecurity measures. Despite the substantial initial cost, Maria weighs the potential ramifications of a data breach against the benefits of robust security measures. By managing the risk of cyber attacks, Maria aims to safeguard sensitive patient information, preserve the pharmacy's reputation, and avoid costly legal fees and fines. The benefits of investing in cybersecurity far outweigh the potential costs of a breach, making it a top priority for the allocation of resources.

Operational Measures: With operational risks posing a significant threat to daily business operations and customer satisfaction, Maria evaluates the proposed investment of $35,000 to implement a reliable pharmacy management system and a robust backup solution. By streamlining operations, improving efficiency, and minimizing downtime, Maria anticipates significant long-term benefits, including enhanced customer satisfaction, increased revenue, and improved brand reputation. Loyalty is vital for sustained business success. Considering the challenges of acquiring and retaining customers in a competitive market, Maria believes that the investment in operational measures will strengthen HealthFirst Pharmacy's position as a trusted community pharmacy, driving long-term growth and profitability.

Compliance Measures: While compliance risks carry lower impact and likelihood compared to cybersecurity and operational risks, Maria recognizes the importance of maintaining regulatory compliance to avoid potential fines and legal repercussions. With the proposed investment of $3,000, Maria is considering implementing compliance management software, conducting regular audits, and providing employee training on data protection protocols. Despite the relatively modest investment, Maria views compliance measures as essential for upholding the pharmacy's integrity and credibility within the healthcare industry. By proactively addressing compliance requirements, Maria aims to mitigate the risk of non-compliance and safeguard HealthFirst Pharmacy's accreditation and reputation.

Moreover, Maria collaborates closely with her Managed Services Provider (MSP) to finalize the decision-making process and allocate budget resources effectively. Together, they prioritize investments based on the severity of risks, available budget, and phased rollout strategy. Recognizing the critical nature of cybersecurity, Maria allocates a significant portion of the budget to strengthen security measures, followed by investments in operational efficiency and compliance management. By adopting a phased approach to implementation, Maria ensures that resources are allocated strategically, maximizing the impact of each investment while minimizing disruption to daily operations. Through careful deliberation and collaboration with her MSP, Maria arrives at a decision that is not only cost-effective but also tailored to address the pharmacy's unique needs and priorities.

Communication and Documentation:

- Maria creates a detailed report outlining the identified risks, associated costs, mitigation strategies, and projected benefits.

- She communicates her findings and decisions to key stakeholders, ensuring transparency and alignment with business goals.

Follow-up and Adaptation:

- Maria understands that risk vs cost analysis is an iterative process.

- She plans to regularly review and update the analysis as HealthFirst pharmacy evolves, ensuring continued alignment with risk tolerance and business objectives.

So, here's Maria showing us how to put a risk vs cost analysis into action for small business decisions. She dives in, looks at all the possible risks, crunches the numbers on costs, and weighs out the best ways to reduce those risks. And voila! She makes a smart investment call that fits right in with her business's plans for growth and smooth operations.

CHAPTER 4

❖

WHAT
SCARES YOU?

totally get that running a business comes with its fair share of worries. You might have had those moments of uncertainty - like the sinking feeling in your stomach when you realize you can't make payroll this month. Or the nightmare scenario of not being able to keep your business wheels turning. Let's not overlook the potential fallout to your reputation if your systems suddenly grind to a halt, leaving your clients stranded and frustrated. These are the raw, palpable fears that can keep you up at night and force you to question every decision. In this chapter, we will talk about the whole "what if" scenarios, confronting the harsh realities of running a business and guiding you through the critical importance of fortifying your operations with robust disaster recovery and data loss prevention strategies.

4.1.
Fear #1:
Losing All Your Data:

Losing important data can be a nightmare for any business owner. The mere thought of losing essential customer lists, financial records, and other crucial documents can cause palpitations. Unfortunately, it's not just a worry but a grim reality.

It's not just cyber-attacks that are a concern for small businesses. Even a simple power outage can lead to data corruption and loss. This is why it's crucial to understand the risks and take steps to safeguard your business. Remember, you don't have to panic. By following some practical tips and investing in the right technology, you can lower the risk of data loss:

1. Keep your software up to date:

Remember, we discussed in the first chapter that when software companies release updates, they often include security patches that address vulnerabilities that hackers could exploit. By keeping your software up to date, you ensure that your system is equipped with the latest security measures, making it less vulnerable to attacks.

2. Use antivirus and anti-malware software:

By installing and regularly updating antivirus and anti-malware software, you can significantly reduce the risk of virus and malware infiltrations.

3. Secure your network:

Begin by implementing a robust firewall. It's like the bouncer at the door, making sure only the right people get in. The firewall diligently monitors and controls incoming and outgoing network traffic, preventing any nefarious attempts to breach your defenses. Additionally, enforce stringent password policies to fortify access points within your network. By having strong passwords and updating them regularly, you add an extra layer of protection, making it harder for unauthorized users to gain entry.

4. Invest in a good backup system:

Regularly backing up your data is essential in the event of a disaster. There are a variety of backup systems available, including cloud backup, external hard drives, and network backup. But here's the kicker: having a backup is only half the battle. It's like owning a bunch of umbrellas but not knowing where they are or whether they've got holes. You wouldn't want to be caught in a downpour only to realize your umbrella is torn and ineffective. Remember, it's all about the three T's: testing, testing, and, you guessed it, more testing! Knowing how to recover is just as important as having the tools in the first place.

5. Train your employees:

Ensure your employees are aware of the impacts of cyber-attacks and provide them with the necessary training to avoid falling victim to a scam. For instance, emphasize the importance of not clicking on suspicious emails or links that may appear scams. Remind them that cybercriminals often use phishing emails to trick individuals into divulging sensitive information or downloading malicious software. Additionally, provide examples of common scams they may encounter, such as phishing emails posing as legitimate organizations requesting personal information or urgent action. Encourage them to verify the authenticity of emails and websites before providing any sensitive data or clicking on links.

6. Work with an IT professional:

Consider enlisting the expertise of an IT professional who can provide you with the most up-to-date insights into data security. Their role is akin to that of a seasoned guide, leading you through the intricate landscape of technology with precision. Consider them your wizards, armed with an in-depth understanding of the intricate tapestry of data security. With their knowledge, they can recommend tailored solutions that align with your business's unique needs. It's like having a compass that points directly to the most secure paths.

4.2.
Fear #2:
Damage to Your Reputation:

In today's digital age, your online reputation holds immense value. A single negative review or social media post can send shockwaves through your business, impacting trust and credibility in an instant. But what happens if your systems fail or your data gets compromised? Your reputation could take a serious hit, potentially tarnishing the hard-earned trust you've built with your customers.

When faced with an IT issue, transparency is key. It's crucial to communicate openly and honestly with your customers about what's happening behind the scenes. Let them know the details of the issue, what steps you're taking to address it, and, most importantly, how you're working to prevent it from happening again in the future.

But it doesn't stop there. To truly safeguard your reputation, you must also address the root cause of the problem. Implementing robust cybersecurity measures, conducting thorough audits of your systems, and investing in employee training are all crucial steps to prevent future incidents.

By prioritizing transparency and accountability in times of crisis, you not only safeguard your reputation but also strengthen the bond of trust with your customers. In an era defined by digital connectivity and instant communication, your reputation is not just a reflection of your business - it's a testament to your commitment to excellence.

4.3.
Fear #3:
Losing Control Over
Sensitive Information

Running a business is like juggling flaming torches while riding a unicycle – a breathtaking performance with a thousand moving pieces. From managing finances and employees to marketing your products and services, it can be a lot to handle. However, one aspect that you cannot ignore is the protection of any sensitive information. With new data privacy regulations in place, you may be feeling the pressure to comply while also worrying about the potential consequences of non-compliance.

It's important to recognize that you are not alone in these concerns. Data privacy is a growing concern for businesses of all sizes, not just in Canada but globally. In today's digital age, customers expect their personal information to be kept safe, and businesses that fail to do so risk damaging their reputation, facing legal consequences, and even losing customers.

To better understand the risks involved, let's take a closer look at the relevant regulations and their implications for your business. In British Columbia, the Personal Information Protection Act (PIPA) outlines the rules for how businesses must collect, use, and disclose personal information. The legislation is designed to balance the needs of businesses to collect and use personal information for legitimate purposes with the right of individuals to have their personal information protected.

To ensure that your business complies with PIPA and other relevant data privacy regulations. Here are some best practices you can follow:

1. Conduct a data privacy audit:

Identify the types of personal information that your business collects, how it's stored, and who has access to it. This will help you determine what changes need to be made to ensure that your processes comply with the law.

2. Implement strong security measures:

Make sure that your data storage systems are secure and that you have proper authentication and encryption in place to protect against unauthorized access.

3. Train your employees:

Make sure that your employees understand the importance of data privacy and how to handle personal information in a way that complies with the law.

4. Be transparent with your customers:

Let your customers know what personal information you collect, why, and how you protect it. This can help to build trust with your customers and increase their confidence in your business.

5. Stay informed:

Data privacy regulations are constantly evolving, so it's important to stay informed of any changes and updates.

With data privacy regulations in place, it's essential to take steps to ensure that your business complies. By following best practices and staying informed, you can minimize the risks associated with non-compliance and ensure that your customers' personal information is kept safe.

4.4.
The Key to Conquering Your Fears

Well, there is a common thread that ties all your fears together, and that is: having a business continuity plan (BCP) in place. Having a BCP means that you have a strategy in place for dealing with the worst-case scenarios, whether it's a data breach, system failure, or any other IT-related disaster.

Business continuity plans are especially important for small businesses, who may not have the resources to bounce back from a major IT disaster. By investing in it, you're not just protecting your data and systems. You're also protecting your organization and your livelihood.

A continuity plan is your secret weapon against all the nightmares keeping you up at night. It's like having a superhero cape for your business, ready to swoop in and save the day when disaster strikes. And trust me, it's not just about backing up your files and crossing your fingers. It involves a comprehensive strategy that includes risk assessment, disaster recovery procedures, crisis communications, and continuity of operations. It's about ensuring that your business can continue functioning even in the face of adversity. From identifying critical business functions and resources to establishing alternative work locations and communication channels, a robust BCP covers all bases to keep your business running smoothly.

Now, when it comes to BCPs, they're as unique as snowflakes – no two are exactly alike. Business continuity planning is highly individualized and varies greatly from one organization to another. However, safeguarding data is a universal concern for all organizations, regardless of size or industry. By emphasizing data security and resilience within your BCP, you can minimize the risks associated with data loss and ensure the uninterrupted flow of your business operations. Here are some general guidelines to help you fortify your data defenses and keep your business running smoothly:

4.4.1. Prepare Your Disaster Recovery Plan.

Organizations must create a solid Disaster Recovery Plan (DRP) that incorporates Recovery Time Objectives (RTO) and Recovery Point Objectives (RPO) to reduce risk and ensure quick uptime in the event of a data loss. Now, I know I just threw some jargon your way, so let's break it down into bite-sized pieces.

RTO specifies how quickly your IT services and infrastructure must be restored after a disaster to maintain company operations. For instance, if your RTO is set at four hours, you should be able to go on with regular business operations within this period in the event of a crisis. Think about the following while calculating RTO:

- The cost per outage hour
- The significance and order of different systems
- The procedures needed to recover after a disaster (including individual components and processes)
- Resources and funds that are readily available.

Now, let's talk about RPO - your data's guardian angel. RPO determines the maximum tolerable amount of data that the business can bear to lose in the event of a disaster. Additionally, it helps organizations determine the time difference between the most recent data backup and a disaster without substantially harming the overall operations. RPO helps you figure out how frequently to back up your data. For instance, let's say your organization operates from 9 am to 5 pm. Suppose a tragedy strikes at 3 pm, and you back up your data once daily at 6 pm. In this scenario, you would potentially lose 6 working hours' worth of data (from 9 am to 3 pm). If your RPO in this situation is 8 working hours (equivalent to 24 hours), meaning you can afford to lose data from the entire day, then you might be adequately prepared for such incidents. However, if your RPO is, say, 2 hours, indicating you can only tolerate a maximum data loss of 2 hours, then you're not adequately covered in this case.

Now that you know how crucial it is to calculate your RPO, here are a few variables that can help you in determining it:

- The maximum amount of data loss that your company can tolerate.

- Cost of data loss.

- The time required to recreate the lost data and resume operations.

- Resources and money that are available.

Being in this field for years now, I know how important it is for your business to know its RTO and RPO. So, I have added an easy-to-access calculator link here that can help you derive your numbers. Check it out:

https://www.itisin.ca/Recovery-time-calculator/check.html

4.4.2. Consider More Than Simply Your Office's Computers.

Preparing your business continuity plan is not just about backing up your servers and devices; it's about ensuring every aspect of your operations is protected. Take a moment to think about all the critical information scattered across your office – from servers and laptops to portable devices and cloud storage.

For instance, have you thought about your website? It's the digital face of your business, but what if it suddenly goes down due to a technical glitch? Do you have a plan in place to swiftly restore it to full functionality?

And what about the data stored in the cloud? While cloud services like Office 365 offer convenience and accessibility, they're not immune to data loss. I have seen many business owners mistakenly believe that because their email is in the cloud, it's automatically backed up. But the truth is, without a proper backup strategy in place, you could be at risk of losing critical emails, files, and communications in the event of a disaster.

Take, for example, the scenario of a cyberattack that compromises your email system. Without a backup, you could face the nightmare of corrupted mailboxes, lost data, and irreversible damage to your business's communication channels.

That's why it's essential to include all aspects of your digital infrastructure in your business continuity plan. Whether it's backing up your website, securing data stored in the cloud, or implementing email backup solutions, every measure you take strengthens your ability to withstand and recover from unforeseen disasters. After all, in today's digital landscape, a comprehensive BCP is your best defense against the unpredictable nature of business interruptions.

4.4.3. Give The Utmost Importance to Crucial Data.

Place paramount importance on critical data within your organization. It's imperative to assess the level of risk associated with potential data loss and tailor your business continuity plan accordingly. Typically, your most vital assets include databases and accounting files, which are the lifeblood of your operations.

Consider implementing a backup schedule that aligns with the importance of these assets. For instance, for businesses heavily reliant on their databases and financial records, hourly backups may be necessary to minimize the risk of significant data loss. Non-profit organizations that frequently input data should prioritize backups after each substantial data entry session to safeguard against potential disruptions.

By recognizing the significance of your crucial data and adapting your continuity plan to prioritize its protection, you're taking proactive steps to mitigate the impact of potential disasters on your business operations.

4.4.4. Ensuring the Preservation and Security

In your business continuity plan, it's imperative to prioritize redundancy and resilience. A robust strategy involves creating multiple copies of your critical data. Ideally, you should maintain three copies of your data, with one copy serving as the production data and the remaining two acting as backup copies.

It is crucial to vary your storage methods to enhance the robustness of your plan. Store these backup data copies in two different formats and ensure they're kept in separate physical locations. This dual-format, dual-location setup shields your data from a wide array of risks, spanning from hardware malfunctions to major disasters.

Additionally, enforce strict access controls to protect your backup copies. Make sure that no single user account can access both backup copies simultaneously to alter or delete any of the backed-up data. This precautionary measure prevents accidental or intentional tampering, bolstering the integrity and reliability of your continuity plan.

4.4.5. Test Your Backups, Before You Need Them

Before you find yourself in a crisis, it's crucial to test your backup plans thoroughly. One crucial aspect of this testing is read-back verification. Read-back verification is a process used to confirm the integrity and completeness of your backed-up data. After data has been backed up, you retrieve a sample of the backed-up data and compare it to the original to ensure it has been accurately and completely copied.

Additionally, a good practice is to create a recovery strategy and test it by transferring a few files to a different computer in a different location before you actually need to use it. The following tests should be performed with your backup solution:

- **Test backup speed:** This test helps you understand how quickly your data can be backed up and restored. It's like timing how long it takes to make a copy of a document and then checking how long it takes to retrieve that copy when you need it.

- **Application backup test:** Let's say you have an important app on your phone. If you accidentally delete it, you want to make sure you can reinstall it and that all your data is still there. This test checks whether your backup plan can successfully restore important applications and their data.

- **Image-based backup test:** Image-based backup involves capturing a complete snapshot of your system, including the operating system, applications, configurations, and data, as a single image. During an image-based backup test, you verify that the backup can be virtualized in a test environment. This involves checking if the entire system environment can be restored accurately and functions as expected. By doing this, you ensure that everything is accurate and operational.

- **Off-site restore test:** This evaluates three critical aspects: firstly, whether the data can be restored from a remote or cloud location; secondly, the time taken to retrieve the data; and finally, the accuracy of the restored data. This test is essential to ensure that your data can be recovered promptly, accurately, and seamlessly, regardless of the location.

Remember, establishing a regular testing schedule is crucial. The frequency depends on the type of backup you're using. For instance, for image-based backups, consider checking daily screenshots, weekly file restores, monthly local virtualization (especially after major updates), and bi-annual or yearly off-site virtualization.

You'll never feel confident in your planning for disaster recovery without routine testing. If you don't have faith in your capacity to recover from failures, you risk experiencing devastating repercussions such as financial losses, damaged client relationships, and reputational harm. I remember an incident from my early career days when a Non-profit organization contacted us to perform their backup restoration after some hardware failure. They had a well-written backup procedure, and they were confident they had a great backup in place, and we thought it was going to be a quick fix. But, when we jumped into it, we found out no data had been backed up for the past three years. No one in their organization has ever tested whether the backup was working before, and it turned out that they lost the last 3 years of data, which resulted in something they couldn't recover from. They shut their doors permanently just a few months later. This is the type of risk I am trying to make you aware of!

The impact of a disaster extends far beyond data loss alone - it can disrupt essential services, impede customer access, and severely affect business operations. Take, for example, the London Drugs cyber-attack, where all 79 stores across B.C., Alberta, Saskatchewan, and Manitoba were shut down for over a week, leaving customers struggling to access prescriptions and other medical needs. Following the cyber-attack, the organization faced challenges in restoring all systems promptly.[7] Such incidents can lead to financial losses, damage to client relationships, and reputational harm. Therefore, businesses must have comprehensive backup plans in place, encompassing not only data protection but also strategies for maintaining operational continuity in the face of unforeseen events. By regularly testing your backup plans and ensuring comprehensive coverage, you can mitigate the risks associated with data loss and operational disruptions, safeguarding your business against potential disasters.

Now that you understand the critical importance of testing your backups, it's essential to recognize that this is just one piece of the puzzle in your comprehensive

---

7   https://bc.ctvnews.ca/london-drugs-president-warns-that-cyber-attackers-constantly-probing-for-weaknesses-1.6880452

business continuity strategy. To truly conquer your fears and fortify your organization against potential disasters, it's imperative to test your entire continuity plan rigorously. This means going beyond just verifying the integrity of your backups and conducting thorough assessments of your recovery strategies, crisis communications protocols, and operational continuity measures. Remember the cautionary tale of the non-profit organization that faced devastating consequences due to an untested backup system. Testing your plan isn't just about ensuring data integrity; it's about safeguarding your business's ability to function effectively in the face of adversity. So, don't overlook this critical aspect of business continuity planning - regular testing is your shield against the unpredictable and your key to conquering your fears.

CHAPTER 5

❖

ESSENTIALS:
YOUR ORGANIZATION CAN'T AFFORD TO OVERLOOK

In today's interconnected world, where digital innovation continues to reshape industries and revolutionize how we operate, it's essential to recognize the inherent risks that come with this technological advancement. While it may be tempting to dismiss these risks, especially for small business owners who historically felt immune, the reality is starkly different. Cybercriminals have evolved, becoming more sophisticated and relentless in their pursuit of targets. Shockingly, statistics reveal that nearly half of all cyberattacks are now aimed at small businesses[8]. This unsettling trend underscores the urgent need for vigilance and proactive security measures.

But why would cybercriminals target small businesses, you may wonder? The answer lies in the valuable trove of data that organizations of all sizes possess. From customer information to financial records, this data represents a lucrative opportunity for exploitation. Moreover, small organizations often lack the robust security infrastructure of their larger counterparts, making them prime targets for cyber intruders.

As our reliance on technology grows, so does the ever-looming threat of cyberattacks. The consequences of a breach can be significant, with the average cost of a

---

8 https://www.getastra.com/blog/security-audit/small-business-cyber-attack-statistics/#:~:text=month%20to%20cybersecurity.-,Small%20businesses%20are%20the%20most%20likely%20to%20receive%20malicious%20emails,to%20these%20businesses%20is%20malicious.

data breach can sometimes reach jaw-dropping amounts. And here's an eye-opener: the average downtime cost for small and medium-sized businesses is $ 8,000 per hour. This amount encompasses the expenses of data and equipment restoration as well as the loss of productivity and revenue caused by the outage.[9]

Understanding the strategies employed by cybercriminals, whether casting a wide net or employing targeted attacks, is essential for fortifying your organization's defenses. By staying informed, implementing robust security protocols, and prioritizing a security-first mindset, small businesses can navigate the intricate landscape of cyber threats with confidence.

Moreover, recognizing the significance of cybersecurity practices goes beyond being a mere suggestion - it's a critical aspect of safeguarding your organization against ever-evolving threats. It's not just about installing antivirus software and hoping for the best; it's about adopting a proactive approach to protecting your organization's sensitive data and assets. So, here are a few key considerations that will undoubtedly benefit your organization in the long run.

---

9   https://www.gggllp.com/the-hidden-costs-of-a-data-breach-for-small-and-medium-size-businesses/

5.1.
Essential Password
Protocols

As a frequent internet user, you must be well aware of the necessity of robust passwords to secure your online accounts. However, remembering different passwords for each account can be a daunting task. That's why modern web browsers offer a feature to store your login information, making it easier for you to log in without the hassle of remembering all your credentials. But did you know that this convenience comes with a significant security risk?

Passwords are sensitive information that can expose your data and services to various threats. Compromised credentials are one of the leading causes of significant data breaches, and with the world becoming more dependent on the Internet, this risk is only increasing. While the time-saving feature of storing your login information might seem like a tempting option, it's important for you to understand the potential risks that come along with it.

When it comes to browser-stored passwords, there's a delicate balance between convenience and security. This vulnerability is evident across popular browsers like Google Chrome, Mozilla Firefox, and Microsoft Edge - all of which manage password storage with usability in mind, sometimes at the expense of robust security.

The main issue stems from the predictable location where browsers store passwords. Despite encryption protocols, the encryption key is often stored nearby, making it susceptible to exploitation. Interestingly, browsers exploit this vulnerability to enhance user experience. They offer features to import saved data, including passwords, from other browsers, which further amplifies the risk.

However, cybercriminals are quick to exploit this weakness. They deploy specialized malware, often referred to as password stealers, which specifically target the folders containing browser-stored passwords. These malicious programs exploit the easily accessible encryption key to decrypt passwords, which are then harvested and sold on the dark web, highlighting just how sophisticated cyber threats have become.

This is where password managers come in. Using a password manager is a more secure solution for generating and storing passwords. Password managers can generate unique passwords for different websites, solving the problem of remembering long passwords while providing strong and unique passwords for all your accounts. By using a password manager, you can reduce your exposure footprint and avoid the risk of all your credentials being kept in insecure locations.

5.1.1. Complex Passwords vs. Passphrases

In the ongoing debate over generating the strongest password, the choice between complex passwords and passphrases has been a hot topic for decades. But let's break it down in simple terms: both serve as passcodes, strings of characters designed to safeguard your accounts. The key distinction lies in how they're constructed.

Traditional passwords consist of random assortments of letters, numbers, and characters, often challenging to recall. On the flip side, passphrases offer a more user-friendly approach, comprising meaningful sentences that are easier to remember. Now, longer passwords generally enhance security against brute force attacks, where hackers systematically try every possible combination of characters to crack passwords. Let's be realistic - it's impractical to expect users to memorize a string of 30 randomly generated characters for each account. And this is precisely where passphrases swoop in to save the day. They provide that perfect balance - long enough to boost security, yet not so complex that you're left scratching your head.

Think about it. Instead of trying to memorize a string of random characters, you could create a passphrase like "Summer is here! Let's hit the beach" or "Coffee fuels my mornings! #JavaLover." Catchy, easy to remember, and, more importantly, secure.

But hold on, before you rush off to update all your passwords, here's a little reality check. Not every application out there supports lengthy passphrases. That's where password managers ride in on their digital white horses. These nifty tools generate unique passwords for each of your accounts, sparing you the headache of memorization. By generating unique, randomized passwords for each account, these tools eliminate the need for memorization while significantly bolstering security. So, while you secure your password manager with a robust passphrase, you can let it handle the heavy lifting of creating and managing unique passwords for every login, minimizing your risk exposure in the process.

Before discussing the intricacies of password strength, let's pause for a moment to understand the stark reality of cyber threats. Remember how I mentioned brute force attacks earlier in this chapter?

Well, brute force attacks are like the relentless bulldozers of the cyber world. They systematically and tirelessly try every possible combination of characters until they hit the jackpot - your password. It's not about wit or cunning; it's all about raw computational power churning through endless combinations.

Now, here's where it gets scary. With today's lightning-fast computers and fancy hardware, attackers can zip through billions of password combos in no time. And if your password is weak - short, simple, or lacking complexity - well, you're basically handing them the keys to the kingdom.

The adjoining image illustrates just how quickly these attackers can brute force your password based on various factors like password length and complexity[10]. I'm showing you this not to scare you but to emphasize just how crucial it is to take your passwords seriously. Gone are the days when 'password123' sufficed; it's time to fortify your digital defenses with stronger, more resilient passwords.

---

10   https://www.hivesystems.com/password-table

TIME IT TAKES A HACKER
TO BRUTE FORCE YOUR PASSWORD

Number of Characters	Numbers Only	Lowercase Letters	Upper and Lowercase Letters	Numbers, Upper and Lowercase Letters	Numbers, Upper and Lowercase Letters, Symbols
4	Instantly	Instantly	3 secs	6 secs	9 secs
5	Instantly	4 secs	2 mins	6 mins	10 mins
6	Instantly	2 mins	2 hours	6 hours	12 hours
7	4 secs	50 mins	4 days	2 weeks	1 month
8	37 secs	22 hours	8 months	3 years	7 years
9	6 mins	3 weeks	33 years	161 years	479 years
10	1 hour	2 years	1k years	9k years	33k years
11	10 hours	44 years	89k years	618 years	2m years
12	4 days	1k years	4m years	38m years	164m years
13	1 month	29k years	241m years	2bn years	11bn years
14	1 year	766k years	12bn years	147bn years	805bn years
15	12 years	19m years	652bn years	9tn years	56tn years
16	119 years	517m years	33tn years	566tn years	3qd years
17	1k years	13bn years	1qd years	35qd years	276qd years
18	11k years	350bn years	91qd years	2qn years	19qn years

Hardware: 12 x RTX 4090   Password hash: bcrypt

IT ISIN
SOLUTIONS

5.1.2. Your common password mistakes.

Let's face it, we've all been guilty of using passwords that are a little too predictable. Whether it's based on family names, hobbies, or a simple pattern, these passwords might be easy to remember, but they're also the least secure. Let's explore some of the most typical password errors and how to fix them.

- Password: zacary12rick5

You might think: "Who could ever guess my password? It's just my kids' names and ages."

Problem: This password relies too heavily on personal information.

Solution: Opt for a stronger version with symbols, uppercase letters, and a more random arrangement. Instead of family names, use unconventional combinations like a character from a movie paired with a type of food. For example, "The Sea Beast" and "pizza" could become "Th3s3aB34stP!ZZa."

- Password: w3St!

You might think: "My password is simple! It's just the beginning of my street address with an extra character."

Problem: This password is too short, with only five characters, and includes part of your publicly available address.

Solution: Strengthen it by making it longer, ideally with more than 12 characters. You can also substitute a nearby street name for your current address. For instance, "Arlington Avenue, Centretown" could become "Rl!ngtOnAv3nu3c3ntr3tOwn."

- Password: BrAveh3av3nD!2

You might be reassured, thinking: "I use the same passwords for all my accounts. It's easier to remember!"

Problem: While there's nothing inherently wrong with this password, using the same one for multiple accounts is risky.

Solution: Create a unique password for each of your online accounts.

Now, let's dive into some best practices to ensure your passwords are as secure as possible:

DOs:

- Make your passwords long and complex, as illustrated in the chart above. Adding more characters and combinations enhances security against brute-force attacks.

- Utilize spaces in passwords where allowed.

- Employ a combination of characters, including capitalization, numbers, and special characters.

- Consider using passphrases instead of

passwords, such as "Aren't beavers cute, awesome, and number 1 in the nation?"

- Ensure each account has a unique password. Yes, every single one! Using the same password for multiple accounts is akin to having one key that opens every door.

- Implement multi-factor authentication, especially for accounts containing sensitive data. I will give more insights about it further in this chapter.

- Utilize password managers to securely store passwords without the need to remember them.

- Change your passwords regularly, ideally every 3 months.

DON'Ts:

- Avoid using repeated characters like "111111111111" or "aaaaaaaaaaaa."

- Steer clear of dictionary words.

- Refrain from using information in passwords that can be easily found on your social media profiles, such as birthdays, anniversaries, or pet names.

- Avoid using obvious passwords like "12345678," "qwerty," or "password."

- Never share your password with anyone.

Remember, your password is the first line of defense against cyber threats, so it's crucial to take password security seriously and avoid falling into the trap of using weak or predictable passwords.

5.2.
Multi-Factor Authentication: Adding Layers of Security

Now that we've covered the fundamentals of password security let's talk about an additional layer of protection: multi-factor authentication (MFA). You may have encountered MFA in various forms, from receiving a code on your phone to using biometric identifiers like fingerprints or facial recognition. But what exactly is MFA, and why is it essential for safeguarding your accounts?

At its core, multi-factor authentication combines two or more independent credentials to verify a user's identity. These factors typically fall into three categories: something you know (like a password), something you have (such as a mobile device), and something you are (biometric data). By requiring multiple factors for authentication, MFA significantly enhances security, making it more challenging for unauthorized users to access your accounts.

So, why is MFA crucial for protecting your online presence? Consider this scenario: even if a cybercriminal manages to obtain your password through phishing or a data breach, they will still need access to your secondary authentication method to gain entry to your account. This additional layer of verification acts as a formidable barrier, preventing many common hacking techniques.

5.2.1. How Can You Implement MFA In Your Organization?

The journey to implementing MFA in your organization might seem overwhelming, but with a systematic approach, it becomes manageable. Here's a detailed guide to help you through the process.

1. Assessing Your Needs

Before starting with the MFA implementation, it's crucial to understand your specific security needs. Start by conducting a risk assessment to identify:

- **Types of Sensitive Data:** Determine what kind of sensitive data you handle. This could include customer information, financial records, or intellectual property.

- **Critical Systems and Applications:** Identify which systems and applications require protection. Typically, this includes email systems, customer databases, and any platforms that handle transactions.

- **User Access Requirements:** Understand who needs access to these systems. Consider the roles and responsibilities within your organization and the level of access required for each role.

2. Compatibility Check with Existing Systems

Before diving into MFA implementation, the first checkpoint is assessing your existing systems' compatibility with MFA. Start by determining if your current systems support MFA. If they do, investigate whether they have their own built-in MFA capabilities or if they can seamlessly integrate with third-party MFA solutions. While many modern applications and platforms are designed to support MFA integration, there can be variations in compatibility based on specific configurations or versions. Conducting a thorough compatibility check ensures that the MFA solution will integrate smoothly without causing disruptions to your operations. I would also recommend consulting with your IT team or your managed service provider (MSP) to verify compatibility and address any potential compatibility issues proactively.

3. Choosing the Right MFA Method

Selecting an MFA method involves evaluating different options based on your organization's needs, budget, and existing infrastructure. Here are some popular ones to consider:

- **Authenticator Apps:** These are smartphone applications like Google Authenticator or Microsoft Authenticator that generate time-based one-time passwords (TOTP). They work by synchronizing with a server and generating a new code every 30-60 seconds, which users input along with their regular password for authentication. Microsoft Authenticator, in particular, offers additional functionality, such as sending a notification to your phone where you can simply approve the login. Authenticator apps are user-friendly, widely compatible with various platforms and services, and provide an additional layer of security beyond passwords.

- **SMS-Based Authentication:** In this method, users receive a one-time code via SMS to their registered mobile number, which they then enter along with their password for authentication. While SMS-based authentication is convenient and doesn't require additional apps or hardware, it's considered less secure than other methods due to potential vulnerabilities in SMS delivery, such as interception or SIM swapping attacks. Interception is like someone sneaking into the middle of a conversation between you and your phone carrier or between your phone and the network. They grab hold of that SMS with your authentication code before it even reaches you. Now, SIM swapping is a bit sneakier. It occurs when an attacker convinces a mobile carrier to transfer the user's phone number to a SIM card under their control, allowing them to receive the authentication code instead.

- **Biometric Solutions:** These include fingerprint scanners, facial recognition systems, and voice recognition. Biometric solutions offer high security since they're inherently tied to the user's physical traits, making them difficult to replicate or steal. However, implementing biometric authentication may require additional hardware (such as fingerprint scanners or cameras) and integration with existing systems.

- **Hardware Tokens:** These are physical devices used for authentication that generate one-time codes or provide touch-based authentication methods, ensuring high-security standards. Examples of hardware tokens include key fobs, smart cards, and USB tokens. These devices require users to possess them physically to authenticate access, making them less susceptible to remote attacks like phishing or hacking. However, they can be costly to implement and distribute to users, and their physical nature may pose logistical challenges, especially for large organizations with dispersed users.

4. Integrating the MFA

Integration can be a complex process, depending on your current systems and the chosen MFA solution. Here's how to approach it:

- **Configuration and Setup:** The next phase includes configuring and setting up the MFA solution according to your organization's requirements. This typically involves collaborating closely with your IT team or MSP to implement the necessary configurations, such as updating software, adjusting user access controls, and defining authentication methods. Depending on the complexity of your systems and the chosen MFA solution, this process may require careful planning and coordination to ensure a seamless transition.

- **Pilot Testing:** Before full deployment, run a pilot test with a small group of users. This helps identify any issues and allows for adjustments before rolling out MFA across the entire organization.

5.2.2. Best Practices for MFA Deployment

Deploying multi-factor authentication is not

just about technology - it's a strategic process that involves engaging your employees and continuously improving your security measures. Here are some key best practices to keep in mind:

- **Employee Training and Awareness:** Your employees are the frontline of your cybersecurity defense, so it's important to ensure they understand the importance of MFA. Communicate why MFA matters, both for the organization and for safeguarding their personal information. Hands-on training sessions are invaluable, allowing employees to familiarize themselves with MFA tools through walkthroughs, video tutorials, and Q&A sessions. Regular updates keep everyone in the loop about any changes or improvements to the MFA system, ensuring ongoing proficiency.

- **Regular Updates and Testing:** Cyber threats evolve constantly, which means your defenses need to keep pace. Keep your MFA software and associated applications up to date with the latest security patches and features. Regular testing and audits help identify vulnerabilities and ensure the MFA system is functioning optimally. Establishing a feedback mechanism encourages employees to report any issues or suggest improvements, contributing to continuous refinement.

- **Comprehensive Implementation:** While it might be tempting to apply MFA only to the most sensitive systems, it's best to deploy it comprehensively across all critical systems. This includes email accounts, cloud services, remote access solutions, and internal applications handling sensitive data or critical operations.

- **Monitoring and Reviewing MFA Logs:** Continuous monitoring is essential for detecting and responding to potential threats. Configure alerts for unusual login attempts, such as multiple failed logins or logins from unfamiliar locations, and consider working with managed service providers or cybersecurity experts who have experience in MFA deployment. They can help set up these alerts and assign a dedicated team or individual to regularly review MFA logs for any signs of suspicious activity.

5.3.
Securing Network
and Endpoint Devices

Network and device security involves protecting all the digital connections and devices that your organization uses. This means making sure that the data traveling across your network, as well as the computers, smartphones, and other devices used by your employees, are safe from hackers and malware.

Let's break down the key components of network and device security and how you can implement them.

- **Firewalls**

Remember our talk about firewalls in previous chapters? Let's focus on them a bit more. A firewall is a security device that monitors and controls incoming and outgoing network traffic. It acts as a barrier between your internal network (trusted) and external networks (untrusted), such as the Internet. Think of it as a security guard that checks who is trying to enter or leave your network. Firewalls come in two main types: hardware and software.

  - **Hardware Firewalls:** These are devices that sit between your internal network and the Internet. They examine all incoming and outgoing traffic, blocking anything that doesn't meet predefined security criteria. Hardware firewalls are an excellent choice for all businesses because they provide robust protection without requiring much technical expertise to set up.

o **Software Firewalls:** Software firewalls run on individual devices, such as computers or servers. They provide an additional layer of protection by monitoring traffic specific to that device. Software firewalls are especially useful for laptops and remote workers who connect to your network from different locations.

It's essential to configure your firewall correctly to ensure it's providing effective protection. Most firewalls come with default settings that offer a good level of security, but you may need to adjust them based on your organization's specific needs. Regular updates are also crucial to keep your firewall defenses up to date against new threats.

o **Intrusion Detection and Prevention Systems (IDPS)**

An Intrusion Detection System (IDS) monitors your network for suspicious activity and potential threats. When it detects something unusual, it alerts you so you can take action. An Intrusion Prevention System (IPS) takes this a step further by automatically blocking or mitigating detected threats.

There are various IDPS solutions available, ranging from simple software to advanced systems. Some IDPS tools focus on detecting threats, while others also include prevention capabilities to automatically block suspicious activity.

When implementing an IDPS, it's essential to configure it correctly to minimize false positives (alerts for harmless activity) and false negatives (failing to detect actual threats). Regular monitoring of alerts and logs is critical to ensure your IDPS is effectively protecting your network.

o Network Segmentation

Network segmentation means dividing your network into smaller parts, each with its own security controls. This way, if a hacker gets into one part, they can't easily access the rest.

Segmenting your network involves creating separate virtual networks, or segments, using your network equipment's settings. You can then apply different security policies to each segment based on its level of sensitivity. For example, you might have one segment for your public Wi-Fi network, another for your employees' devices, and a third for your servers containing sensitive data.

Network segmentation helps control breaches by limiting the impact of an attack. Even if a hacker gains access to one segment, they won't necessarily be able to move laterally to other parts of your network. It also allows you to apply more stringent security measures to your most critical assets while maintaining flexibility for less sensitive areas.

o **Endpoint Security**

Endpoints are the devices that connect to your network, such as computers, smartphones, and tablets. Securing these devices is critical because they are often the entry points for cyber-attacks.

Endpoint security encompasses a range of measures designed to protect individual devices from cyber threats. Here are some key strategies:

o Install reputable antivirus and anti-malware software on all devices. This software detects and removes malicious programs that can harm your system. Remember to schedule regular scans to identify and eliminate threats. Additionally, ensure the software is set to update automatically to protect against new threats.

o Keeping your operating systems, applications, and firmware up to date is essential. Remember our discussion back in Chapter 1 about how software updates often come with patches for security vulnerabilities? These patches are crucial because they fix weaknesses that attackers could exploit. I would strongly suggest you implement a policy that ensures all devices are regularly updated.

o You can consider implementing EDR solutions to monitor endpoint devices for security threats. EDR continuously collects and analyzes data from all endpoint devices - such as desktops, laptops, mobile phones, and IoT devices - to detect suspicious activities and potential breaches in real-time. With capabilities like automated threat response, threat isolation, and remediation, EDR helps identify, respond to, and mitigate cyber threats efficiently. EDR systems provide security teams with detailed information and visibility into endpoint activities, facilitating quick and effective responses to security incidents. Implementing EDR solutions to monitor endpoint devices for security threats. EDR continuously collects and analyzes data from all endpoint devices - such as desktops, laptops, mobile phones, and IoT devices - to detect suspicious activities and potential breaches in real-time. With capabilities like automated threat response, threat isolation, and remediation, EDR helps identify, respond to, and mitigate cyber threats efficiently. EDR systems provide security teams with detailed information and visibility into endpoint activities, facilitating quick and effective responses to security incidents.

In addition to EDR, integrating MDR services into your endpoint security strategy can significantly enhance your organization's cybersecurity posture. MDR services combine advanced technology with human expertise to offer continuous monitoring, threat hunting, and rapid response to detected threats. These services leverage EDR tools for enhanced threat detection and analysis, ensuring a comprehensive defense against cyber threats such as ransomware, malware, advanced persistent threats (APTs), and insider threats. MDR is particularly beneficial for organizations that may lack the in-house resources or expertise to manage their security operations, providing 24/7 monitoring and incident response from a skilled security team.

5.3.1. Strategies for Effective Network and Device Security

Now that you understand the basics of network and endpoint security, let's understand how you can implement these measures in your organization.

- **Assessing Your Network and Devices**

Let's say you're the owner of a small retail business. You have a few computers at your storefront for inventory management and sales transactions, as well as a shared printer and separate Wi-Fi networks for customer and internal use. Here's how you can assess the security of your network and devices:

1. Inventory Check: Begin by creating an inventory of all devices connected to your network. This includes computers, printers, Wi-Fi routers, and any other internet-enabled devices. Don't forget to account for devices brought in by employees or vendors, such as smartphones and tablets. It is possible that you discover that an employee has connected their personal laptop to the store's Wi-Fi network without your knowledge. This unauthorized device could pose a security risk if it's not properly secured or if it introduces malware to your network.

2. Risk Assessment: Once you have a comprehensive list of devices, assess the security risks associated with each one. Consider factors such as outdated software, weak passwords, lack of encryption, and physical vulnerabilities. For instance, you realize that your point-of-sale (POS) system is running on outdated software with known vulnerabilities. This puts your customers' payment information at risk of being compromised by cybercriminals.

3. Vulnerability Remediation: Develop a plan to address any vulnerabilities you identify during the assessment. This may involve installing software updates, strengthening passwords, enabling encryption, or implementing physical security measures.

- **Developing and Enforcing Security Policies**

Security policies serve as the foundation of your cybersecurity strategy. They outline the rules and guidelines that govern how employees should use company devices and access network resources. Here's how you can develop and enforce effective security policies:

1. Clearly Define Rules: Start by creating comprehensive policies that cover all aspects of network and device security. Clearly outline rules regarding password management, data access controls, software usage, and acceptable internet browsing behavior. Additionally, guidelines for the use of personal devices on the company network must be specified.

2. Train Your Employees: Conduct regular training sessions to educate your employees about these policies and the importance of adhering to them. Ensure that employees understand the potential risks associated with non-compliance

and the role they play in safeguarding company assets and data. Provide examples of security best practices and demonstrate how to implement them in day-to-day tasks.

3. Enforce Policies Consistently: Consistent enforcement of security policies is essential for maintaining a secure environment. Utilize monitoring tools to track compliance and identify any deviations from established guidelines. Implement measures to address non-compliance promptly, such as issuing warnings, providing additional training, or imposing disciplinary actions when necessary. Regularly review and update security policies to adapt to evolving threats and technology advancements.

5.3.2. Common Challenges and How to Overcome Them

Implementing network and device security can be challenging, but understanding these common hurdles can help you overcome them.

• **Challenge:** User Resistance

Employees might resist new security measures if they perceive them as inconvenient or unnecessary.

Solution: Educate your employees on the importance of security and how it protects both the business and their personal information. Provide clear instructions and support to make the transition smoother.

- **Challenge:** Cost

Small businesses often have limited budgets for cybersecurity.

Solution: Start with the basics, like firewalls and antivirus software, which are relatively inexpensive. Look for scalable solutions that can grow with your business.

- **Challenge:** Technical Complexity

Implementing advanced security measures can be technically complex, especially for small businesses without dedicated IT staff.

Solution: Seek help from managed service providers or cybersecurity consultants. They can offer expertise and support to ensure your security measures are correctly implemented and maintained.

5.4.
Cybersecurity Training and Awareness for Employees

While you may have invested in various security measures like antivirus software and firewalls, it's essential to recognize that your employees play a crucial role in protecting your business from cyber threats. But are they equipped with the knowledge and awareness needed to defend against cyberattacks?

When we discuss the human factor in cybersecurity, we're highlighting the significant role that people play in either enhancing or undermining your organization's security measures. Despite the advancements in technology and security solutions, humans remain susceptible to manipulation and exploitation by cybercriminals. Here are some common scenarios where the human factor comes into play:

- Phishing Attacks: These attacks are like the digital version of a con artist's sleight of hand. Imagine receiving an email that appears to be from a legitimate source, such as your bank, a colleague, or a well-known organization. The email may contain urgent requests or enticing offers, prompting you to click on links or provide sensitive information like login credentials, credit card numbers, or personal details.

Cybercriminals use sophisticated techniques to make these emails appear genuine, especially with advancements in AI, which have become easier to accomplish and often mimic the branding and language of trusted companies. They exploit human emotions like curiosity, fear, or greed to manipulate recipients into taking actions that compromise security. Unfortunately, phishing attacks are prevalent and can have devastating consequences if successful.

- Social Engineering Tactics: This involves manipulating individuals into divulging confidential information or performing actions that compromise security. These tactics rely on human psychology and the tendency to trust others. Cybercriminals may impersonate authority figures, such as IT technicians or company executives, to gain access to sensitive systems or data.

For example, an attacker might call, posing as a helpdesk technician, and convince an employee to reveal their login credentials under the guise of troubleshooting a technical issue. Alternatively, they may exploit personal relationships or shared interests to establish rapport and extract sensitive information.

- Weak Password Practices: We've already touched on the importance of strong password practices in this chapter, but it's worth reiterating the role of weak passwords in exposing your business to security risks. Using weak passwords or reusing the same password across multiple accounts can create vulnerabilities that cybercriminals can exploit.

These scenarios highlight just a few ways in which human behavior can either bolster or weaken your cybersecurity defenses. To protect your business effectively, it's crucial not only to invest in robust technological solutions but also to ensure that your employees are well-trained and vigilant. Cybersecurity training and awareness programs are essential in fostering a security-conscious culture within your organization. By educating your staff on the latest threats and best practices, you empower them to act as an integral part of your cybersecurity strategy.

5.4.1. How to Develop an Effective Training Program?

Creating an effective cybersecurity training program involves careful planning and execution. Here's a step-by-step guide to getting started:

1. Assess Your Training Needs:

Before you can design a training program, it's crucial to understand your current cybersecurity knowledge and identify areas where your employees might need additional support. This assessment can take various forms:

- Cybersecurity Knowledge Assessment: Start by evaluating your employees' current understanding of cybersecurity concepts. This can be through quizzes or surveys about things like spotting phishing emails, creating strong passwords, and understanding social engineering tactics.

- Gap Analysis: Identify any gaps or weaknesses in your current cybersecurity practices or knowledge. Are there specific areas where your employees consistently struggle or where your organization is particularly vulnerable to cyber threats?

- Feedback from Employees: Don't forget to solicit feedback from your employees themselves. They may have insights into areas where they feel less confident or where they believe additional training would be beneficial.

1. **Set Clear Objectives:**

Once you know where you need to improve, set clear goals for your training program. What do you want to achieve? Some possible objectives could include:

- Identify and Report Phishing Emails Accurately: One of the most common cybersecurity threats for small businesses is phishing attacks. Your objective might be to increase employees' awareness and vigilance in identifying and reporting phishing attempts.

- Improving Password Security Practices: Weak passwords are another common vulnerability.

Your objective could be to improve password security practices by encouraging employees to use strong, unique passwords and enabling two-factor authentication.

- Increasing Overall Cybersecurity Awareness: Ultimately, you want to create a culture of cybersecurity awareness within your organization. Your objective could be to increase employees' overall understanding of cybersecurity risks and best practices.

2. Choose the Right Delivery Methods:

Once you've defined your objectives, you need to choose the delivery methods that will be most effective for your employees. Consider factors such as:

- Learning Preferences: Different employees may have different learning preferences. Some may prefer in-person workshops or interactive online courses, while others might prefer self-paced learning modules or short videos. Try to accommodate a variety of learning styles.

- Accessibility: Ensure that your chosen delivery methods are accessible to all employees, regardless of their location or technical expertise. This might mean offering both online and offline options or providing training materials in multiple languages.

- Engagement: Choose delivery methods that will engage your employees and keep them interested and motivated. Gamification, real-life examples, and interactive quizzes or activities can all help make your training program more engaging.

3. Measure Your Success:

Finally, don't forget to measure the effectiveness of your training program. This allows you to track progress, identify areas for improvement, and demonstrate the value of your investment in cybersecurity training. Some ways to measure success include:

- Quizzes or Assessments: Administer quizzes or assessments before and after the training program to measure improvements in knowledge and understanding.

- Monitoring Security Incidents: Keep track of the number and type of security incidents reported by employees. Ideally, there should be no instances of falling for attacks, but what matters most is your starting point and observing a decline in instances over time.

- Surveys and Feedback: Gather feedback from employees about their experience with the training program. What did they find most valuable? What could be improved? Use this feedback to refine and enhance future training initiatives.

Cybersecurity is a constantly evolving field, with new threats emerging regularly and new solutions being developed to counteract them. As a result, a single training program is not enough. Your employees need to be continually educated and reminded of best practices to keep your organization secure. This requires a commitment to ongoing learning and adaptation.

Regular updates to your training program are essential. As new threats emerge, your training content should be updated to reflect the latest information and techniques. This ensures that your employees are always equipped with the most current knowledge and skills.

Moreover, it encourages a culture of continuous improvement and learning. Make it clear that cybersecurity is a priority for your business and that everyone has a role to play in maintaining security. By fostering an environment where employees feel responsible and empowered to contribute to cybersecurity, you can create a more resilient organization.

5.4.2. Implementing Ongoing Awareness Initiatives

Cybersecurity awareness is not a one-time event but an ongoing process that requires regular reinforcement and communication. Here are strategies for maintaining awareness:

- Regular Communication: Keep employees informed about cybersecurity risks, emerging threats, and best practices. You can use various communication channels, such as newsletters, emails, and updates on the company intranet, to disseminate this information. For example, you could send out a monthly cybersecurity newsletter highlighting recent security incidents, tips for staying safe online, and reminders about company policies.

- Phishing Simulations: Conduct regular phishing simulations to test employees' awareness and responsiveness to phishing attempts. Provide feedback and additional training based on the results of these simulations. This practice helps reinforce the training and keeps employees vigilant.

- Reward and Recognition Programs: Everyone loves a little recognition for their hard work, and cybersecurity is no exception. Implementing a reward and recognition program can incentivize employees to prioritize cybersecurity practices. Consider recognizing employees who demonstrate exemplary cybersecurity practices, such as reporting suspicious emails or completing cybersecurity training modules. You can offer rewards such as gift cards, extra time off, or public acknowledgment at company meetings. By highlighting positive cybersecurity behaviors, you reinforce the importance of security within your organization and motivate others to do the same.

- Incident Response Drills: Conducting regular incident response drills and tabletop exercises can help ensure that your employees are ready to handle real-world cyber threats effectively. These drills simulate various cybersecurity scenarios, such as a ransomware attack or a data breach, and allow employees to practice their roles and responsibilities in a controlled environment. For example, you could simulate a phishing attack that results in a compromised system and task employees with identifying and containing the threat. By practicing their response procedures regularly, employees become more familiar with the steps to take during a cybersecurity incident, reducing response times and minimizing the impact of the incident.

5.5.
The Untold Reality
of Cyber Insurance

As cyber threats continue to evolve and proliferate, the concept of cyber insurance has gained traction among organizations seeking protection from potential financial losses. However, amidst the marketing hype, small business owners must grasp the nuanced reality behind cyber insurance.

Cyber insurance, in essence, is a policy designed to mitigate financial losses resulting from cyber incidents. It promises to cover expenses related to data breaches, ransomware attacks, and other cyber threats. It is often portrayed as the solution to all your cyber security problems. However, the truth is that cyber insurance is not a reasonable solution to the security threats faced by small organizations. Let's talk about the facts to help you make an informed decision.

One of the most overlooked aspects of cyber insurance is the prerequisite for robust cybersecurity measures. In recent years, insurance companies have raised the bar, demanding detailed insights into the security protocols and defenses employed by businesses seeking coverage.

Insurers scrutinize businesses with a fine-tooth comb, probing for evidence of proactive cybersecurity measures. From firewalls to encryption protocols, businesses are expected to demonstrate a comprehensive approach to cybersecurity before they can even be considered for coverage. Unfortunately, this means that if you haven't implemented reasonable security measures, it will be almost impossible to get cyber insurance coverage.

As the frequency and sophistication of cyber-attacks continue to escalate, insurance companies are tightening their belts, becoming increasingly selective about whom they deem worthy of coverage. For small businesses, this spells trouble. Without the financial resources of their larger counterparts, securing cyber insurance coverage can feel like an uphill battle.

So, where does this leave small organizations? In navigating the treacherous waters of cyber security, it's essential to adopt a holistic approach. While cyber insurance may have its time and place, it should never be viewed as a substitute for robust cybersecurity measures. Instead, organizations should focus on fortifying their defenses, investing in employee training, implementing robust security protocols, and staying abreast of emerging threats.

CHAPTER 6

CHALLENGES FACED BY ALL SMALL ORGANIZATIONS

I magine standing at the edge of a high-wire tightrope, balancing multiple plates on long sticks, with each step forward feeling precarious. This metaphor perfectly encapsulates the daily life of a small business owner. You're the marketer, the customer service rep, the financial officer, and the tech expert—all rolled into one. I know that you face unique and daunting challenges that can often feel like navigating a labyrinth with shifting walls.

From keeping up with the rapid pace of technological advancements to safeguarding against ever-evolving cyber threats, the road to success for small organizations is fraught with obstacles. But fear not! This chapter is your guide through the maze, offering practical insights and advice to help you conquer the challenges and emerge stronger and more resilient.

We'll talk about the top challenges small organizations face today and, more importantly, how you can tackle them head-on. By understanding these hurdles and learning how to overcome them, you can transform potential roadblocks into stepping stones for growth and success.

6.1.
Challenge: Keeping Up with
Rapid Technological Change

Technology is an ever-changing landscape that can be a double-edged sword for small organizations. On the one hand, advancements in technology can be a boon for your organization, but on the other hand, it can also be a significant challenge to keep up with the latest trends and innovations.

To succeed in today's competitive market, it's crucial to embrace new technologies and stay ahead of the curve. By doing so, you can streamline your business processes, improve customer experiences, and ultimately increase your income.

But what are some of the biggest challenges that small businesses face when it comes to keeping up with technology? Let's take a closer look.

- *Cost:* Every dollar you spend needs to count towards growing your organization and achieving your goals. However, when it comes to investing in new technologies, it can be difficult to justify the cost. After all, there are so many other expenses to consider, and it can be tempting to put off investing in new technology until you have more cash flow.

But here's the thing: investing in new technology can save you money in the long run. By streamlining your processes and improving efficiency, you can reduce costs and increase profitability. For example, investing in software that automates certain tasks can free up time and resources that you can allocate towards other important areas of your organization. And with the right hardware and infrastructure in place, you can ensure that your team is working at peak performance, which can translate into higher productivity and revenue.

It's also worth noting that investing in new technology can help you attract new customers and retain existing ones. Today's consumers expect organizations to have a strong online presence and to offer a seamless digital experience. By investing in the right technologies, you can create a user-friendly website, streamline your online ordering process, and provide exceptional customer service. All of these factors can help you stand out from the competition and build a loyal customer base.

- *Lack of expertise:* Another challenge is the lack of expertise and technical knowledge within small organizations. While it's true that investing in training and hiring IT professionals can be costly, it's important to consider the long-term benefits. By having a team with the technical expertise to manage your systems, you can avoid costly downtime, improve productivity, and stay ahead of the competition. It may also be worthwhile to consider outsourcing your IT needs to a managed service provider, which can provide expert support and guidance without the cost of hiring a full-time IT team.

- **Time constraints:** It's important to prioritize and make time to learn about new technologies. Consider setting aside dedicated time each week to research and stay informed about emerging trends and advancements related to your industry. This can include reading industry publications, attending webinars or workshops, or networking with other business owners to share knowledge and insights.

It's also important to recognize that you don't need to become an expert in every new technology that comes along. Instead, focus on identifying the technologies that are most relevant to your business and explore ways to integrate them effectively. Don't be afraid to seek outside help when needed, whether that means hiring a consultant or partnering with a technology provider.

6.2.
Challenge:
Managing Data

One of the biggest challenges that small organizations face when it comes to data management is simply having too much information to keep track of. From customer and vendor contact information to financial records and sales data, there's no shortage of data that you need to keep organized and accessible.

One way to tackle this challenge is by implementing a comprehensive data management system. This might include using customer relationship management (CRM) software to store and organize customer information or using accounting software to manage financial records. With so many software options available, it's essential to choose the one that best fits your business needs. For instance, Freshbooks, Xero, and QuickBooks are popular accounting software choices among small organizations.

6.3.
Challenge: The Need for Up-to-Date Security Measures

With the increasing amount of sensitive information being stored and transmitted online, it's becoming increasingly critical to have up-to-date security measures in place. Cybercriminals see small businesses as easy targets since they often have less robust security systems in place. Additionally, small businesses are often less equipped to handle the aftermath of a cyberattack, which can lead to devastating consequences, including loss of sensitive information, financial damage, and even permanent closure.

So, what can you do to protect your business from these types of attacks? The first step is to educate yourself about the different types of cybersecurity threats, including malware, phishing scams, and network intrusions. You should also make sure that you have a backup of all your sensitive data in a secure location. This will allow you to recover quickly in the event of a cyberattack.

Next, you need to implement strong security measures, such as firewalls, antivirus software, and Managed Detection and Response. Remember, we discussed these in the previous chapter! These technologies can help protect your business against cyberattacks and prevent sensitive information from being stolen. Additionally, you should have a plan in place to respond to a cyberattack, including steps to take to mitigate the damage and recover quickly.

It's also important to stay up to date with the latest security technologies and best practices. This means regularly reviewing your security systems and making sure that they are in line with current standards. You can also attend cybersecurity training sessions and workshops to learn more about how to protect your business.

I'm sure you're wondering if all this talk about security is worth the effort. And to be honest, it can be a lot of work. Ensuring your business is well-protected against cyber threats takes time and money. But the alternative is much worse. Without proper security measures in place, you run the risk of facing a costly cyberattack. Small businesses, in particular, are vulnerable and can suffer significant losses. It's not uncommon for them to face bills of over $100,000 following an attack. For some, this can be the final straw, leading to permanent closure.

6.4
Challenge: Which Cloud-based Solutions to Choose?

The growth of the Internet and mobile devices has changed the way we do business, and cloud computing has become an increasingly popular solution for organizations of all sizes. However, with so many options available, it can be challenging to determine which cloud-based solutions are right for you and your business.

Essentially, cloud computing refers to the delivery of computing services over the Internet, providing on-demand access to servers, storage, databases, networking, software, analytics, and intelligence. This means that you don't have to worry about the hassle of purchasing, maintaining, and updating expensive hardware and software. Instead, you can access these services as needed and pay only for what you use.

Cloud computing has been on the rise for several years now, and for good reason. It is driven by factors such as increased demand for cloud-based solutions, the need for remote work capabilities, and the rise of digital transformation initiatives. But what does this mean for small businesses in particular? Well, it means that you can save money by paying only for what you use rather than investing in expensive hardware and software. It also provides you with greater flexibility and scalability, allowing you to quickly adapt to changing business needs. Additionally, it increases your security and reliability, as cloud providers typically invest heavily in their infrastructure and security measures.

To determine which cloud-based solutions are right for your business, you'll want to consider your specific needs, such as data storage, data management, and collaboration tools. For instance, if you need a way to store and manage your data, cloud-based solutions like Microsoft Sharepoint or Google Drive might be worth considering. Conversely, if you require a way to collaborate with your team, solutions like Microsoft Teams or Google Meet may be more suitable.

Embarking on the cloud computing journey can be both exciting and daunting. It's a powerful tool that can help your business grow and evolve. The first step is to comprehend your business requirements and determine which cloud-based solutions can best meet those needs. This may involve consulting with IT experts or conducting research on your own.

Once you have a better idea of what you need, the next step is to choose a reliable cloud provider. With so many options out there, it can be overwhelming to decide which one is right for you. Popular cloud providers like Amazon Web Services (AWS), Microsoft Azure, and Google Cloud Platform offer a range of solutions that cater to different needs. But remember, when selecting a provider, you should consider factors such as security, reliability, scalability, and cost. It's also important to evaluate the level of support and resources available, such as documentation, training, and customer service.

Migrating to the cloud is a process that requires careful planning and coordination. It's important to involve key stakeholders, such as IT staff, in the decision-making process to ensure a smooth transition. And while it may take time to fully integrate cloud-based solutions into your business operations, with patience and dedication, you can successfully reap the benefits of this transformative technology.

6.5.
Challenge:
Integrating Systems and
Applications

As your organization grows, you'll likely need to integrate different systems and applications to streamline your operations. However, integrating these systems and applications comes with several challenges, and cost is one of the biggest. Implementing new software or applications can be expensive, and integrating them with your existing systems can add even more cost. This can be especially difficult for small organizations with limited resources to invest in new technology, making it challenging to keep up with the latest developments.

Compatibility is another challenge to consider. Not all systems and applications are designed to work together seamlessly, and even those that are compatible may require customization to integrate effectively. This can be time-consuming and frustrating, especially if you're not familiar with the technical details of your systems.

To overcome the challenges of integrating your systems and applications, it's essential to have a clear understanding of your needs and goals. Start by identifying the systems and applications that are critical to your business and determine how they can work together to support your operations. Next, research the available options and consider factors like compatibility, cost, and ease of use for each option. Additionally, it's always a good idea to seek advice from experts if you need help with the technical aspects of integration.

6.6.
Challenge:
Staying Ahead of Cyber Threats

Staying ahead of the game has always been crucial for any business owner. However, in today's digital age, there is an even more pressing concern that you need to be aware of: cyber threats. With the majority of business conducted online, it's vital that you take proactive measures to protect yourself and your customers from potential cyber-attacks.

So, what exactly are cyber threats? Simply put, they are any type of malicious activity or attack that occurs over the Internet or other digital networks. This can range from phishing scams and hacking attempts to viruses and malware. The primary objectives behind these attacks typically involve financial gain through the theft of sensitive information, such as personal or financial data, by disrupting the normal operations of networks or devices or by deploying ransomware to extort money from victims in exchange for restoring access to their encrypted data.

Now, why should you be concerned about cyber threats? For starters, cyber-attacks are becoming increasingly common. In Canada, the number of reported cyber-attacks continues to rise every year, and this trend doesn't seem to be slowing down anytime soon. As more devices become connected to the Internet and online transactions become more prevalent, the risk of cyber threats also increases.

Moreover, cyber security incidents can have significant financial implications. Organizations affected by cyber-attacks tend to allocate significantly higher budgets toward prevention and detection measures compared to those that have not faced such threats. On average, impacted organizations invest $113,000 in enhancing their cyber security defenses. Small businesses impacted by cyber incidents spend 120% more than non-impacted peers, while medium and large enterprises increase their expenditure by 39% and 75%, respectively.[11]

---

11   https://www150.statcan.gc.ca/n1/daily-quotidien/221018/dq221018b-eng.htm

These statistics underscore the importance of taking cyber threats seriously and being proactive in protecting your business from potential attacks. Implementing strong cybersecurity measures and regularly updating your systems can help safeguard your business and mitigate the financial and reputational risks associated with cyber incidents.

If you're a small business owner, it's important to be aware that you're at a higher risk of falling victim to cyber-attacks. Unlike large corporations, you may not have the same level of security measures in place, making you an attractive target for cybercriminals. Sadly, small organizations are often singled out because they are considered easy targets.

The consequences of a cyber-attack can be severe and far-reaching. Losing sensitive data and customer information can be disastrous for both you and your customers. Moreover, the fallout can be expensive and time-consuming to recover from and can also damage your reputation. In some cases, legal repercussions may also arise.

So, what can you do to protect your business from these threats? Here are some steps you can take to stay ahead of cyber threats:

- *Hire a Cybersecurity Expert or a Managed Service Provider (MSP):* A cybersecurity expert or an MSP can conduct a thorough assessment of your systems and identify any potential vulnerabilities, risks, and areas for improvement. They can help you understand the potential impact of a data breach or cyberattack on your business and help you prioritize your security investments.

These experts are trained and knowledgeable in the latest best practices and technologies for securing your systems. They can help you implement these best practices and ensure that your systems are as secure as possible.

Depending on your industry, you may be required to comply with various security regulations and standards. A cybersecurity expert or an MSP can help you understand and meet these requirements, ensuring that you remain compliant and avoid any legal or financial penalties.

- *Be Cautious with Emails and Attachments:* Did you know that emails and attachments can be a gold mine for cybercriminals? It's true! By simply clicking on a suspicious link or downloading an infected attachment, you could be opening the door to all sorts of trouble. From having your identity stolen to losing access to your important files and accounts, the consequences can be severe.

To protect yourself, it's best to approach all emails and attachments with a healthy dose of caution. Here are some tips to keep in mind:

- o Be skeptical of emails from unknown senders or those with strange subject lines. Cybercriminals often use convincing language and logos to lure unsuspecting victims into clicking on malicious links or downloading infected attachments. If an email sounds too good to be true or too urgent, it's important to take a moment to think twice before taking any action. Be wary of any email that asks you to disclose personal information or login credentials, as this is often a sign of phishing.

- o Don't click on any links or download any attachments until you've verified the sender's identity and the content is safe. Before clicking any links in an email, hover your mouse over them to see the actual URL. This can usually be seen at the bottom of your email client or web browser. If the email seems legitimate but you have doubts, contact the sender through alternative means to confirm the authenticity of the message.

o Keep your security software up to date, as this can help prevent malware from infecting your devices and keep your personal information safe. Antivirus programs, firewalls, and other security tools are essential for protecting your devices from cyber threats. It's important to regularly check for software updates and install them as soon as they become available.

o If you receive an email with an attachment or link that you're not sure about, reach out to the sender to confirm it's legitimate before taking any action. Don't be afraid to ask questions, and make sure that the email is really from the person or organization it claims to be from. If you can't verify the message, it's always better to err on the side of caution and delete it.

- **_Conduct Regular Security Audits:_** Think of it like a spring cleaning for your digital life. Just like how you go through your closet to see what you need to keep, toss, or donate, a security audit helps you identify and fix any potential security holes in your systems and devices.

A security audit is an important process to assess the security of a system or network. The purpose of a security audit is to identify vulnerabilities and risks that could potentially compromise the confidentiality, integrity, or availability of the system. During a security audit, a cybersecurity expert or your MSP evaluates your current security measures and recommends improvements to mitigate these risks. They also evaluate the effectiveness of your network's perimeter defenses, such as firewalls, intrusion detection systems, and other security devices. They analyze network traffic and examine logs to look for signs of suspicious activity, unauthorized access attempts, or malware infections.

Another critical aspect of a security audit is reviewing the patching and software update procedures for your systems. The experts ensure that all software, applications, and operating systems are up to date with the latest security patches and that any known vulnerabilities are addressed.

6.7.
Challenge: Adapting to the Mobile Revolution

It's no secret that mobile technology has revolutionized the business world. Gone are the days when customers were limited to shopping during store hours or accessing services only when physically present. Today, consumers are glued to their mobile devices, and they expect organizations to meet them where they are

- on the go. As a small business owner, you may be feeling the pressure to keep up with this new mobile-first world. And it's understandable - adapting to these changes can be overwhelming. But rest assured, you're not alone. Many other small organizations are facing the same challenges, and there are strategies you can employ to stay ahead of the curve.

One key strategy is to ensure that your website and online presence are optimized for mobile devices. This means designing your website with mobile users in mind so it's easy to navigate and use on a smaller screen. You can also consider developing a mobile app to make it even more convenient for customers to interact with your business.

Another important factor is to stay up to date on the latest mobile trends and technologies. For example, the rise of mobile payments and mobile wallets has made it easier than ever for customers to make purchases using their mobile devices. By staying informed and adapting your business accordingly, you can stay ahead of the competition and provide a better overall customer experience.

So, while the mobile revolution may seem daunting at first, there are plenty of resources and strategies available to help you succeed in this new landscape. With the right approach, you can not only meet but exceed the expectations of today's mobile-first consumers.

6.8.
Challenge:
Managing Remote Teams

The trend towards remote work has been growing rapidly in recent years, particularly in response to the COVID-19 pandemic. While this shift has brought many benefits to businesses and employees, it has also presented new challenges, particularly for small businesses. One of the biggest challenges is managing remote teams, as the lack of face-to-face interaction and the need for virtual communication can create barriers to productivity and engagement.

However, with the right approach, organizations can effectively manage remote teams and overcome these challenges. Key strategies include:

- **Investing in Communication and Collaboration Tools:**

One of the most important steps for organizations looking to manage remote teams effectively is to invest in communication and collaboration tools. These tools are designed to facilitate virtual interaction and teamwork, ensuring that remote teams stay connected, informed, and on track.

One example of a powerful tool is Slack, a popular chat app that allows team members to communicate in real-time, share files, and collaborate on projects. Slack also integrates with a wide range of other tools, such as Google Drive and Trello, making it an ideal platform for remote teams.

Another effective collaboration tool is Microsoft Teams, a platform that offers a range of features, including instant messaging, audio and video calling, and file sharing. Microsoft Teams also includes tools for project management and teamwork, making it a comprehensive solution for small businesses looking to manage remote teams.

- **Establishing Clear Guidelines and Expectations:**

In addition to investing in these tools, organizations also need to establish clear guidelines and expectations for their remote teams. This includes outlining the responsibilities of each team member, setting specific goals and objectives, and establishing protocols for communication and collaboration.

For example, an organization can set clear guidelines for when and how team members should be available for virtual meetings, as well as expectations for response times to emails and other forms of communication. You might also establish protocols for how team members should handle urgent situations and what the protocol is for communicating with the team when they are not working.

- **Regularly Checking in with Remote Team Members:**

To keep your remote team running smoothly, it's essential to maintain regular communication with your team members. By frequently checking in with your remote employees, you can ensure that everyone is on the same page and working towards common goals.

Regular check-ins can also help you to identify any potential issues early on, allowing you to take proactive steps to address them before they become major problems. This could include discussing any challenges team members may be facing, addressing any questions or concerns they may have, and providing feedback on their work.

To ensure that your check-ins are effective, it's important to establish clear communication channels that everyone can access easily. This could include video conferencing, instant messaging, or email, depending on your team's preferences and needs.

To further support your remote team members, you can also offer regular training sessions. These sessions can help team members stay up to date on the latest tools and strategies for virtual collaboration. By investing in your team's skills and knowledge, you are enabling them to work more efficiently and effectively, no matter where they are working from.

CHAPTER 7

❖

MAKING THE RIGHT CHOICES

Your organization is a bustling hive of activity. Every minute counts, and every task completed efficiently contributes to your success. But what if I told you that hidden inefficiencies in your IT systems could be costing you more than just time? **What if your staff could work one week a year for free, simply because of IT inefficiencies?**

Let's say your organization has 10 employees, and each employee loses 10 minutes daily due to slow or inefficient computer systems. The impact on productivity is significant.

Here's the math:

Daily Loss: 10 employees x 10 minutes = 100 minutes lost per day

Weekly Loss: 100 minutes x 5 days = 500 minutes lost per week

Annual Loss: 500 minutes x 52 weeks = 26,000 minutes, or approximately 433 hours of lost productivity per year

This means each employee is losing about 43.3 hours of productivity annually due to inefficient computer systems. If you think about it, this translates to over one whole week of lost productivity per employee annually!

By optimizing your IT systems, you could reclaim this lost time, effectively giving your team an extra week of productive work each year. This not only boosts your team's efficiency but also enhances your overall business performance. Let's discuss how you can achieve these savings and improve your operational efficiency.

7.1.
Choosing the
Right Hardware

Selecting the right hardware is fundamental to building a reliable and efficient IT infrastructure for your organization. Hardware encompasses the physical components of your IT setup, including computers, servers, networking equipment, and peripherals. Let's explore how to make informed decisions that align with your business needs.

- **Performance vs. Cost:** Balancing performance and cost is essential when selecting hardware. Cutting-edge technology offers top-tier performance but might not always fit within your budget. Conversely, cheaper options could compromise long-term reliability and efficiency. The key is to evaluate your specific needs and future growth projections to determine the right level of investment.

- **Scalability:** Small organizations are dynamic entities that evolve over time. Your chosen hardware should be capable of scaling alongside your business. Investing in scalable solutions ensures that your IT infrastructure can accommodate increased workload demands, additional users, and technological advancements without requiring frequent upgrades or replacements. While scalable hardware may have a higher initial cost, the ability to upgrade components incrementally will save costs associated with purchasing entirely new systems as your business grows.

- **Compatibility:** In the rapidly evolving world of technology, it's crucial to invest in hardware that not only supports current technologies but is also adaptable to future advancements. Here are steps to ensure compatibility of your new hardware with existing systems:

  1. *Inventory Current Systems:* Document the specifications and configurations of your existing hardware and software.

  2. *Research Compatibility:* Check the compatibility of new hardware with existing systems. Consult vendor documentation and support forums.

3. ***Pilot Testing:*** Before a full-scale rollout, test new hardware in a controlled environment to ensure smooth integration.

- **Durability and Reliability:** These are key considerations, particularly for hardware that will be used frequently or in demanding environments. Investing in durable hardware can reduce the need for frequent replacements and minimize downtime. For example, if a critical laptop fails and it takes a week to find the right configuration, set it up, install apps, integrate, and then hand it over, consider the impact on productivity. Can you afford to be without your device for a week? If your laptop dies, the cost isn't just the replacement cost but also the lost productivity.

Therefore, it's crucial for the organization to assess which devices are critical and cannot afford downtime. These devices should be prioritized for investment in durable and reliable hardware. On the other hand, less critical devices could be considered for bulk spare purchases or less robust models to optimize budget allocation without compromising essential operations.

I would advise you to look for products with high durability ratings and positive user reviews. Additionally, opt for products with comprehensive warranties and strong manufacturer support.

Durable hardware may have a higher upfront cost, but the extended lifespan and reduced maintenance needs often result in a lower total cost of ownership (TCO).

Choosing the right hardware for your organization is a critical decision that impacts productivity, employee satisfaction, and operational efficiency. Remember the wisdom from chapter one: "I am not rich enough to buy cheap things." The right hardware is an investment in your organization's future, paving the way for a more efficient, productive, and profitable operation.

7.2.
Choosing the
Right Software

In today's digital age, the software choices you make can dramatically influence your business's efficiency, productivity, and overall success. While hardware forms the foundation of your IT infrastructure, software is the engine that drives daily operations. The right software solutions can streamline workflows, enhance communication, and provide the data insights needed to make informed decisions. However, with countless options available, how can small business owners like you make the right choices? Let me help you with that question!

Selecting software tailored to your organization's unique needs requires a thoughtful approach. It's not just about picking the most popular or the most affordable option; it's about finding tools that integrate seamlessly into your existing processes or help upgrade your processes to be more efficient, empowering your team to perform at their best. Let's talk about the key considerations for choosing the right software:

- **Identifying Business Needs:** The first step in choosing the right software is to clearly identify your organization's specific needs and challenges. This involves a thorough analysis of your current operations and pinpointing areas where software can drive improvements.

Start by mapping out your existing workflows and identifying bottlenecks or inefficiencies. For example, if your team spends an inordinate amount of time managing customer inquiries, a robust customer relationship management (CRM) system could streamline these interactions and free up valuable time. You can look for tools tailored to managing customer relationships, tracking interactions, and providing valuable insights that can enhance customer satisfaction and retention.

Engage your employees in the decision-making process. After all, they are the ones who will be using the software daily. Solicit their feedback on current pain points and gather suggestions for potential solutions. This collaborative approach ensures that the selected software addresses real issues and has the buy-in of your team, which is critical for successful implementation and adoption.

Additionally, consider not only your current needs but also your future growth. For instance, if you are running a retail business and you anticipate a significant increase in sales volume, investing in an inventory management system that can handle more extensive data and integrate with your existing platforms will save you from future headaches.

- **Ease of Use:** Even the most powerful software can be a hindrance if it's not user-friendly. Ease of use is a critical factor, as it affects how quickly your team can adapt to and effectively utilize new tools. I would suggest looking for software with intuitive interfaces and straightforward navigation. Complex software can lead to frustration and resistance from your team.

Choose software that offers comprehensive training resources and customer support. This can include tutorials, webinars, and detailed documentation. A vendor that provides excellent customer support can make a significant difference in resolving issues quickly and ensuring that your team can make the most of the software.

Ease of use also involves the ability to customize the software to fit your specific needs. Software that allows you to create personalized dashboards, reports, and workflows can enhance productivity.

- **Integration Capabilities:** Seamless integration with existing systems is essential for maximizing the efficiency of your IT infrastructure. You should look for software solutions that offer robust and secure integration capabilities, ensuring that data flows seamlessly between different applications without compromising the security or integrity of any system involved. This not only minimizes manual data entry but also enhances data accuracy, streamlines workflows, and provides a holistic view of your business operations.

Remember, the software landscape is constantly evolving. Stay informed about new tools and technologies, and be open to adapting your software choices as your organization grows and changes. Regularly review and assess the effectiveness of your current software solutions to ensure they continue to meet your needs.

Ultimately, the right software empowers your team to work smarter, not harder, and positions your organization to thrive in a competitive market.

7.3
Choosing the Right IT Partner

Selecting the right IT partner is a pivotal decision that can significantly influence the efficiency, security, and growth trajectory of your organization. An IT partner not only provides technical support but also offers strategic insights, helps you navigate technological changes, and ensures that your IT infrastructure aligns with your business goals. Now, let's look into how to choose an IT partner that fits your needs:

- **Assessing Service Offerings:** The breadth and depth of services offered by an IT partner should align with your current and future needs. Key service areas to evaluate include:

  o Managed IT Services: Comprehensive management of your IT infrastructure, including proactive monitoring, maintenance, and support.

  o Cybersecurity Solutions: Robust protection against cyber threats, encompassing threat detection, prevention, and incident response.

o Cloud Services: Expertise in cloud computing solutions for scalability, data management, and application hosting.

o IT Consulting: Strategic advice and planning to optimize technology investments and align them with business objectives.

o Business Continuity: Disaster recovery planning and solutions to minimize downtime and ensure data integrity.

Ensure the IT partner has a proven track record in delivering these services.

- **Opting for Proactive Support:** Choose an IT partner that prioritizes proactive support over-reactive responses. Proactive monitoring and maintenance can prevent potential issues from disrupting your operations, allowing you to concentrate on strategic initiatives rather than firefighting IT problems. Look for partners that emphasize continuous monitoring, regular maintenance, and robust security measures to keep your systems running smoothly.

- **Long-term Partnership Focus:** Seek an IT partner interested in building a lasting relationship rather than simply executing one-off projects. A committed partner can provide ongoing support, contribute to your business growth, and act as a trusted advisor for future technology endeavors. Long-term partnerships foster collaboration and enable your IT partner to tailor their services to your evolving needs, ensuring consistent service delivery and responsiveness.

- **Rethinking the Value of Customer Feedback:** To make an informed choice regarding an IT partner, it's essential to go beyond online reviews, which can often be biased or paid for. Instead, prioritize direct conversations with their clients. These discussions offer genuine insights into the IT partner's service quality, responsiveness, and overall client satisfaction. By analyzing feedback patterns that mirror your specific needs - like reliability and exceptional customer support - you can confidently assess their suitability.

- **Making the Final Decision:** After evaluating potential IT partners based on the above criteria, it's time to make the final decision. Here are a few additional steps to ensure you choose the best fit:

  o Request Proposals: Ask shortlisted IT partners to submit detailed proposals outlining their approach, services, and pricing. Compare these proposals side by side.

o Conduct Interviews: Schedule interviews or meetings with the key representatives of each IT partner. Use this opportunity to ask questions, clarify doubts, and gauge their commitment to your business.

Investing time and effort into selecting the right IT partner pays off in the form of increased efficiency, reduced downtime, enhanced security, and, ultimately, a more productive and satisfied team. Remember, the right IT partner isn't just a service provider or a vendor - they are an extension of your business, dedicated to helping you thrive in an increasingly digital world.

As the founder of an MSP (Managed Services Provider) company, I've seen firsthand the critical difference between a vendor and a true partner. Before establishing my business, I worked with a break-fix IT support company serving small organizations in Kamloops. During this time, I observed a common issue among these enterprises - they would only seek IT assistance when faced with a crisis. Unfortunately, this reactive approach often led to high costs, prolonged downtimes, and hindered overall productivity and growth.

Over time, I realized the limitations of that model for small organizations. This led me to establish my MSP company, where I aimed to shift away from the traditional break-fix method that often left business owners in distress. Rather than profiting only when they faced problems, I wanted to create a setup where business owners could operate without worry, knowing their IT needs were consistently supported. This approach ensures that I succeed when my clients succeed, aligning our interests for mutual benefit.

Unlike break-fix services that react to problems as they occur, MSPs like mine offer continuous support, maintenance, and monitoring. This proactive approach ensures that businesses operate smoothly, minimizing disruptions and maximizing efficiency. Today, my company serves as a dependable partner for my clients, enabling them to thrive and achieve their goals.

So, I would strongly suggest that choosing an IT partner shouldn't be about simply purchasing services or products. It should be about selecting a trusted advisor who understands your organization's goals and helps you navigate technological challenges. A proactive IT partner will work alongside you, ensuring your technology supports your growth and success every step of the way.

7.4.
Making the Right Investment:
Business Continuity

As a business leader navigating the complexities of today's digital landscape, you understand that resilience is not just a buzzword–it's a strategic imperative. Business continuity planning is your proactive shield against the unpredictable storms that can disrupt operations, from cyber-attacks to natural disasters. It's about safeguarding your business's ability to weather the unexpected and emerge stronger on the other side.

When considering the investment in business continuity, it's essential to assess the costs comprehensively. Beyond the tangible expenses of backup systems, data storage, and disaster recovery planning lie the intangible costs of downtime, lost productivity, and damaged reputation. These hidden costs can far outweigh the initial financial outlay of a robust continuity plan.

- Preparation Costs: The initial phase of creating a business continuity plan involves conducting a thorough risk assessment and business impact analysis. This foundational step identifies critical functions and vulnerabilities, laying the groundwork for strategic investment. Preparation costs may encompass consulting services to guide this process, acquisition of specialized software and hardware tailored to your needs, and training to empower your team with the necessary skills and awareness.

- Implementation Costs: Once the plan is drafted, implementation involves translating strategy into action. This stage often requires investments in upgrading existing systems, deploying new technologies, and potentially engaging a Managed Service Provider (MSP) for ongoing management. Implementation costs should be viewed as an upfront investment in resilience, positioning your organization to swiftly respond to disruptions without compromising operational continuity.

- Testing and Maintenance Costs: The effectiveness of any business continuity plan hinges on regular testing and maintenance. Simulating disruptive scenarios and evaluating response capabilities ensures readiness when it matters most. Ongoing maintenance involves updating software, hardware, and policies to align with evolving threats and technological advancements. These iterative costs are essential for validating and optimizing your preparedness, minimizing the likelihood and impact of potential disruptions.

- Recovery Costs: In the aftermath of a disruptive event, recovery costs come into play. These may encompass expenses for temporary facilities to sustain operations, costs associated with data restoration and system recovery, and replacement of damaged equipment. By anticipating these recovery expenditures within your continuity plan, you mitigate financial surprises and expedite the path to full operational restoration.

The investment in business continuity is not merely a budget line item—it's a strategic imperative that fortifies your organization's resilience and secures its long-term viability. Consider the lessons learned from recent global challenges, such as the COVID-19 pandemic - One in five B.C. temporarily closed, and one in three operated at reduced capacity[12]. Additionally, 31 percent of B.C. businesses indicate a decline in their performance compared to pre-pandemic levels. Among these, smaller organizations reported more deterioration in their situation compared to larger enterprises[13].

By prioritizing business continuity, you not only safeguard against potential crises but also foster

12 https://www2.gov.bc.ca/assets/gov/employment-business-and-economic-development/business-management/small-business/sb_profile.pdf

13 https://www150.statcan.gc.ca/n1/daily-quotidien/220530/dq220530b-eng.htm

a culture of preparedness and agility within your organization. This proactive stance not only shields against financial losses but also enhances operational efficiency and stakeholder confidence. Ultimately, investing in business continuity is an investment in your organization's ability to thrive in an increasingly volatile and interconnected world.

As you navigate the dynamic landscape of modern business, remember that the cost of preparedness pales in comparison to the cost of unpreparedness. Embrace continuity planning as a strategic asset that empowers your business to navigate uncertainty with confidence, ensuring continuity of service, protection of assets, and preservation of your hard-earned reputation.

Remember, making the right choices in IT isn't just about staying current with technology trends - it's about leveraging technology to propel our organization forward. It's about embracing opportunities, mitigating risks, and building a foundation for sustained success in an increasingly digital landscape. By prioritizing informed decision-making in IT, we lay the groundwork for a resilient, agile, and future-ready organization.

As we look ahead, let's remember that our journey in harnessing technology is not a solitary path but a strategic roadmap toward achieving our business objectives. By making the right choices today, we position ourselves to thrive tomorrow, navigating challenges with confidence and embracing growth opportunities.

CONCLUSION

✤

As we wrap up The IT Survival Guide, it's evident that technology has transitioned from a mere tool to a vital engine of success for small organizations. You now know that when managed effectively, IT is a strategic investment that not only reduces long-term costs and shields your organization from cyber threats but also paves the way for exciting growth opportunities. This guide has equipped you with the insights and strategies needed to confidently navigate the intricate world of IT. Throughout this book, we've identified the common IT missteps that many small business owners encounter and explored how to sidestep them. We've dissected the true costs of IT -both visible and hidden - and highlighted how informed technology choices can lead to significant savings. Moreover, we've addressed the pressing challenge of cybersecurity, providing you with actionable strategies to build a resilient foundation that keeps your organization secure and ready for whatever lies ahead.

IT as a Strategic Investment

Let's reinforce an essential point: IT is not merely an expense; it's a powerful investment. Like any investment, it demands careful planning, attention to detail, and adaptability to evolving circumstances. The organizations that excel in today's competitive landscape are those that utilize technology to not only tackle immediate challenges but also strategically position themselves for sustainable growth and security. Whether it's upgrading outdated systems, investing in cybersecurity, or choosing the right IT partner, every decision you make shapes the future of your organization. Technology can be a powerful asset when aligned with your business goals, and the knowledge you've gained from this guide will help you make informed, impactful decisions going forward.

Moving Forward with Confidence

Now, it's time to put what you've learned into action. Start by assessing your current IT setup: What's working? What needs improvement? Where are the gaps in security or efficiency? Take the time to build an IT roadmap that addresses both your short-term needs and long-term goals, and don't hesitate to consult with

IT professionals who can provide guidance tailored to your business.

As you move forward, remember that technology is constantly evolving, and so should your approach to managing it. Stay informed about the latest trends in cybersecurity, cloud computing, and business continuity. Continuously educate yourself and your team, and be proactive about making adjustments as your organization grows.

Final Thoughts

The world of IT may seem overwhelming at first, but with the right mindset and tools, it becomes an opportunity rather than a challenge. By avoiding common mistakes, cutting unnecessary costs, and securing your organization, you're setting the stage for continued success in a digital world. Your small business is unique, and the right IT solutions can help you unlock its full potential.

You now have the roadmap to make smarter, more secure IT decisions. As you continue to navigate the ever-changing digital landscape, this guide will serve as a reference point, a survival manual to keep your business thriving.

Here's to your success in making IT work for your organization - helping you avoid mistakes, cut costs, and stay secure.